M000017835

INVENT YOUR FUTURE

Endorsements for *Invent Your Future*

"Paul David Walker is exceptionally good at what he does. *Invent Your Future* takes the leadership principles in his *Unleashing Genius: Leading Yourself, Teams and Corporations* to a higher and deeper level. A must read!"
—Joseph F. Prevratil, President and CEO, Archstone Foundation

"The principles in *Invent Your Future* are a palette of vivid colors of intuition and self-discovery. Use liberally to turn your blank canvas into your compelling picture … again and again." —Sandra Berg, CEO, Ellis Paint Company

"*Invent Your Future* is a go-to book. It is packed full of anecdotal information and examples that address our day to day challenges and opportunities."
—Steve M. Rosol, President/CEO, Mars Air Systems

"We invent our future with every decision we make—the wisdom of the leaders speaking through this book empowers us to be mindful and intentional about the future we create." —Katherine Perko, Human Resources Executive

"This is a compelling guide to unleashing the leader within. We cannot create what we cannot conceive, and Invent Your Future is a great tool for leaders that seek to conceive continual growth, both personally and professionally."
—Michael DuRee, Fire Chief, Long Beach, California Fire Department

"Here you will find a treasure trove of distinctions, tools, and models that will allow you to engage people in a way that naturally harmonizes and enhances working with others—and that in turn advances the mission and purpose of the organization. More than that, you will be introduced to the thinking that guides and directs our most advanced leaders. There are years of learning available in *Invent Your Future*. Do not be surprised when, in the days and months to come, you find yourself referencing this book. It's that good."
—John King, Bestselling Author of *Tribal Leadership*

"Paul has been a huge help to me over the several years that we've been working together. He has helped me to understand who I am as a leader. His blend of mental toughness and generous spirit is inspiring and clear. This book is an in-depth exploration of the concepts that Paul has passed on in his work, and will be an excellent reference and reminder. These leadership lessons are invaluable."
—Garson Foos, President, ShoutFactory

INVENT YOUR FUTURE

STARTING WITH YOUR CALLING

By Paul David Walker

HIGHPOINT
EXECUTIVE
PUBLISHING

www.highpointpubs.com

NEW YORK — SAN FRANCISCO

Invent Your Future: Starting With Your Calling
Copyright © 2015 by Paul David Walker

All rights reserved. Published in the United States of America. No part of this book may be reproduced or transmitted in any form or by any means, graphic, electronic, or mechanical, including photocopying, recording, taping, or by any information storage or retrieval system, without permission in writing from the publisher.

This edition published by Highpoint Executive Publishing.
For information, write to info@highpointpubs.com.

First Edition

ISBN: 978-0-9861585-1-3

Library of Congress Cataloging-in-Publication Data

Walker, Paul David
Invent Your Future: Starting With Your Calling

Summary: "Utilizing the insights of twenty successful business leaders interviewed exclusively for this book—CEOs, chefs, city managers, nonprofit directors, and entrepreneurs—author Paul David Walker provides a roadmap that everyone, from from people beginning to plan their lives, to those in the halls of power and influence, can use to achieve higher levels of mastery in the art of inventing the future."—Provided by publisher.

ISBN: 978-0-9861585-1-3 (paperback)
1. Business 2. Philosophy

Library of Congress Control Number: 2015935019

Interior design by Sarah Clarehart
Front cover design by Paul David Walker
Photos taken by Paul David Walker with his iPhone except where noted.

10 9 8 7 6 5 4 3 2 1

Dedication

To all leaders who have the courage to do one of the most difficult jobs in the world.

CONTENTS

Photo: Sarah Clarehart

Acknowledgments

First, I would like to acknowledge all the leaders who have contributed to this book. It would not have been possible without your insights. Of these people, I especially want to acknowledge Larry Senn, founder of Senn Delaney Leadership. Your mentoring and support made much of the success in my life possible. Thanks also to Michael Roney of Highpoint Executive Publishing for your insight and careful guidance, and to Sarah Clarehart for the book design. You have been great partners.

A special thanks goes out to Michael Utvich, who one afternoon inspired me to write this book. What you said to me that day resonated with my heart and soul. Thank you for that and for the continuous guidance during the early writing of the book. I have learned so much from you about book writing, among other things.

I thank each of you who will read this book and invent a better future for yourselves and your families. As you invent your futures, our world will become a better place.

I thank my wife, Bonnie Joy Walker, for the unconditional love and insights that she provides each day. Love is the light of the soul, and yours lights me up every day. Your wisdom has made much of my life both insightful and a joy. Many thanks to my son Yanni Dylan Walker, who has encouraged me by his example as a leader.

Foreword

A funny thing happened on the way to the publication of this book. The world turned upside down, a worldwide recession occurred, and great, glaring deficiencies in our leadership infrastructure were exposed.

In the aftermath of 2008, millions were suddenly brought to the realization that everything they knew was wrong and the old thinking didn't cut it in the new world. After seventeen years of unprecedented productivity in finance, government, business, foreign relations, and even the arts, the party was finally over—and it was over with a bang. The years that followed were not fun, but much was to be learned, especially in the area most lacking—leadership. It was missing, and life had been so easy and generous that we didn't notice that leadership was missing until it was too late.

So, the question is: What have we learned, if anything?

Enter *Invent Your Future*, a handbook for rebooting yourself and your organization.

Paul David Walker is a lifelong student of the art of leadership. He understands that management principles, although vital to the efficient running of any organization, are insufficient when leadership is called for. Above all, as Paul shares with us in this important "field manual," we realize that leadership is a different domain from management. Too often, our great managers fail when they attempt to lead by using accepted business school principles. We call that form of quasi-leadership "management on steroids," and it is exactly what it sounds like: louder, more dominating, and more survival-driven, with behaviors that serve to accelerate the ineffectiveness of the people in the organization. No one works well in an environment dominated by fear.

Paul speaks to the needs of the individual manager who is committed to being an effective leader. In this book, you will find a treasure trove of distinctions, tools, and models that support the kind of leadership that keeps people engaged in their work activity—and in a way that naturally harmonizes and enhances working with others, and forwards the mission and purpose of the organization. More than that, you will be introduced to the underpinnings of the thinking that guides and directs our most advanced leaders.

It is not enough that a book bring tips and tactics to solve particular issues. This book's purpose is to get you to think as a leader and therefore to act as one. This change comes from a deep understanding of what leadership is actually about, and the willingness and courage to implement the principles and distinctions—sometimes in the face of well-intended or not-so-well-intended criticism. Throughout *Invent Your Future*, you will see that a leader is, above all, courageous. This means that the leader is on a very slippery slope and must choose the path between failure to act (cowardice) and overreacting to the situation (recklessness). Many die on this hill.

One of Paul David Walker's great talents is his ability to tell an effective story that moves people to action. This is a fundamental leadership skill that Paul demonstrates repeatedly, and one that every aspiring leader must master. We live in an era of communication. It is no longer sufficient to merely lead by example—a leader must also teach, and teach in a way that allows and inspires the student to turn around and teach as well. The true function of the leader is to create an environment that nurtures the natural leadership capabilities of others. This book is about that in spades: leaders creating leaders.

Invent Your Future is filled with stories about great leaders who have been there, and their inspiring learning experiences about how they thought and acted their way through the many challenges on their plates.

In this book you will see yourself over and over as someone who has the intelligence and the mastery in life to apply these guidelines, and as someone who is "rounding out" his or her business education in leadership, and taking it to a higher level. It is not too much to say that, in the background, Paul is addressing the spiritual quality of leadership in the individual. That's a big deal, and something that is rarely covered in a no-nonsense, hardball book about business leadership.

Read this book through without stopping. Get the gist of the thinking that Paul is offering. Then, re-read it for content, marking the great stories and principles in which you want to ground yourself. There are years of learning available in *Invent Your Future.* Do not be surprised when, over the years ahead, you find yourself referencing this book repeatedly. It's that good.

Invent Your Future will find an honored place in your library of books and literature on the subject on leadership, and you will find yourself returning to certain passages over and over again as the years pass. This information is useful, timeless, and well-proven. For a lot of this, you will be validated—you know more that you think. For some of this, you will be surprised—you don't know as much as you think. Some of you will access a new domain of leadership, and will relaunch your career to a higher trajectory—one of authentic, thoughtful, strategic, and effective leadership.

John King

Author of *Tribal Leadership*

The Journey to Your Future

Imagine those explorers who left the shores of Europe in small wooden ships, venturing out onto mammoth uncharted oceans to discover new lands. They had to be prepared and ready to respond to unexpected realities. Your life is similar. This book will prepare you.

To get the most value from this book, please suspend what you think you know. Leave yourself open to new insights and understandings. You can always return to different parts of the book after you read and reflect. By letting go of all but the lessons of the past, it will be easier to see the correct path as it emerges from the present.

Wisdom often comes from moments of stillness. While you read this book, take time to reflect in beautiful environments that lift your spirits.

My purpose is to help you invent the future you were meant to have, using lessons from those who have succeeded.

My grandfather always said, "Luck is when preparation meets with opportunity." I was born in a lock house, alongside an English canal, where my grandfather lived. The lock house was next to the pump house, which filled the lock after the canal boats entered. Once the water in the lock reached the higher level, the boat would continue its journey. Now I bring people and teams into my lock, raise their level, and they continue on their journeys. This dynamic was magic to me as a young boy, and my grandfather seemed so important. I remember coming down the stairs in the morning, leaving footprints on the wood, which was a little damp. As I moved toward the kitchen I could feel the heat of the coal fire and breakfast cooking. When I wanted to go to the other side of the canal, instead of going way down to the bridge, I would jump on the boats and cross to the other side while being chased by the boatmen.

Grandfather's lock house was surrounded by green plants, which seemed so wise and happy, even though they stood in the heart of industrial England, full of soot. In my memory, that old, simple house still feels like home. As you will see later in this book, early childhood memories often form our passions.

But this life was not good enough for my dad who left for America. He came over first, found a place to live, and then sent for my mother and me. We arrived in New York harbor on the bow of the Queen Mary, full of hopes and dreams, and possessing nothing but suitcases. I remember throwing coins at the Statue of Liberty for luck. I was often told, "Your mom and I came to this country to provide a better future for you." Indeed, my parents set me on a course that has provided success and happiness, but not without some rough seas.

Taking Responsibility for the Future

As my parents and I arrived on American shores, we were keenly aware of needing to invent our future—as a family and as individuals. We came from a land where it was hard to invent anything that transcended our social class, but America was different. We were in an environment that was structured to help people take responsibility and full control of their lives.

The truth is that we all are inventing our futures moment to moment. A word said in anger can reverberate for generations, or a moment of opportunity seen and acted upon can change a life. It is like we are all surfers in the flow of cause and effect. Using our consciousness and intuition we can feel that spot of the wave that maximizes forward progress, and then progress from there. A vortex of energy resonates with our calling. We can ride it to the shore or be washed over in a moment of distraction. We can pick the right wave for our skill, weight, and strength … or the wrong one. When we choose unconsciously we can be driven into the rocks.

Feeling the Flow

By feeling the flow of the moment, you can catch the wave that is just right for you, and invent a future that is an expression of your natural genius. To put it another way, each one of us is a single note in the symphony of life that only we as individuals can play. Playing that note creates a resonance with the orchestra and will infuse you with the energy of the whole.

It is often said that we all have a destiny, yet most do not seem to manifest it. Numerous times I have felt the pull of my destiny, but lost track of it while trying to live up to my father's dream for me. Many of us end up living lives of quiet desperation, anger, and resentment, because we are living someone else's dream, or none at all.

If we are born to manifest our destiny, why does it happen so rarely? There are many reasons. This book shares what I have discovered about manifesting my own destiny, combined with what the CEOs of successful companies have learned about inventing the future of their own lives and businesses.

Thirty Years of Leadership Consulting

Much of what I know about inventing the future came from my work helping build one of the world's top leadership consulting firms, Senn Delaney Leadership. Our mission focused on aligning business strategy, structure, and organizational culture—one of the first such groups to specialize in this approach. I have also worked with many other midsize companies and start-ups. Overall, our client list is long and diverse, including the following:

- New York Life
- StarKist Foods
- Mutual of Omaha
- Anne Klein
- Harrods
- Rockwell International
- Chase
- Conexant Systems
- Union Pacific
- Coach Leather
- Teradata
- Learning Curve Toys

My teachers and mentors include the following:

- Sydney Banks, spiritual teacher and author
- Brugh Joy, spiritual teacher and author
- George Pransky, founder, Psychology of Mind
- Linda Pransky, cofounder, Psychology of Mind
- Christina Davidson, spiritual teacher
- Don Ross, CEO and chairman, New York Life
- Larry Senn, founder and chairman, Senn Delaney Leadership
- Dr. Ellsworth Barnard, professor, Northern Michigan University

In addition to my role as a business consultant, I am also a poet, a mystic, and a storyteller. My purpose is to tell stories—sharing what I have learned and guiding you through practices that will lead you to live the life that has always called you.

Some of the stories in this book are mine, some are from history, and many are from the highly successful leaders I've interviewed for this book—CEOs, chefs, city managers, nonprofit leaders, and everyday people—all of whom are reinventing their lives. Enjoy the glimpses into their worlds. As you do, notice what resonates with you, and the underlying strategies employed. See if you can see their tricks. Write your insights in your journal as you read. It is important to capture your thoughts as they occur—as a resource for knowing yourself.

Everyone, from people beginning to plan their lives, to those in the halls of power and influence, can achieve higher levels of mastery in the art of inventing the future. Doing so not only impacts you as an individual, but can help reinvent the world. If each of us mastered the art of inventing our futures, our world would shine brighter with each generation.

Your Only Real Choice

Given today's volatile economic times, the need to invent your future is the only accountable choice for individuals, leaders, teams, and corporations. No one will do it for you. Knowing how to invent the future will enable you to successfully compete in today's world.

In simpler economic eras, knowing how to invent the future was a strategic advantage; now you need this knowledge to survive. Learning to master your state of mind is key to all kinds of success. In my previous book, *Unleashing Genius: Leading Yourself, Teams and Corporations*, I talk about "Integrative Presence," which is the ability to let go of your thoughts about how you think things are, responding to the actual flow of cause and effect. It is like athletes being "in the zone," responding to the flow of a game instead of thinking about what to do when critical moments could pass them by. Your life and business will be passed by if you don't invent your future yourself.

The Journey and Outcomes

For most of my life I have helped leaders align business strategy, structure and organizational culture. I started in manufacturing in the early 1970s, improving the performance of factories by asking questions, and then synthesizing people's ideas into practical action. Having grown up tending my father's orchards, vineyards, and truck farm, I seem to naturally see a better way. I learned many lessons from growing fruits and vegetables. Land is like a life: the more you tend it with loving care, the richer and more plentiful the fruits.

How do you live happily in this world while inventing a future for yourself, your family, and your business? My dad was an engineer, and he always taught me to first discover the true nature of things, and people.

Using this Book

Each chapter in this book provides stories that resonate with the cords of creation. The Prologue, titled "Leaders' Stories," is packed full of advice from successful self-made leaders. Their perspectives appear in full here. Selected excerpts from each of these perspectives are amplified upon and revisited in subsequent chapters. I add my own reflections and practices that will help you weave their successes into inventing your future. The effects of this reading will build with a series of empowerments that will challenge and lift you. You will gain progressive insights, practices, and a new lens through which to experience in the world—all intended to teach you mastery of the art and science of inventing the future.

This book is supported by external articles and videos that will deepen your understanding of its themes. When you see this link icon 🔗 , go to **www.inventyourfuturebook.com** to view the videos. (E-book readers, you can simply click on the icon each time you see it.)

The Interviews

The perspectives that appear in the Prologue and throughout the book are based on interviews that I conducted with leaders who successfully invented their futures, and those of their businesses or organizations. They all felt a calling that left hints and messages throughout their lives. Those who succeeded heard these messages, and acted on them with courage.

As these people began to resonate with their callings, floods of images revealed possible futures that fit their imaginations and feelings. Once they committed to what they were meant to be, each of them started a process to encourage others to commit to supporting their success in creating a future for the greater good of everyone.

All had high levels of presence—a state in which they could see opportunities and dangers emerging, and they had the courage to act. Some interviewees told me this directly. In others I could feel it—a deep stillness in the storms around them, which contributed to their presence and insight.

The Themes

This book's chapters examine variations of several themes that have emerged from my work with CEOs over the last thirty years.

Know Yourself

Many people have adopted a persona or have designed their lives based on what someone else has told them they should be. Sometimes they have become the opposite. Usually something in the middle is who we truly are. Yet we have all had moments when everything flowed naturally. How do we integrate the lessons of these moments into our life?

Every life has a rhythm and flow. When you become an expression of your own natural genius, you will dance naturally to the rhythm and flow of the moment. Singers hit the top of the charts when they stop copying their idols and find their own voice. One example that comes to mind is Bruce Springsteen, which I discuss in Chapter 1. There are many others as well.

Cheetahs run like the wind, and elephants are strong and powerful. If you are a cheetah, but think you are an elephant, pulling logs from the forest will be difficult. You will never beat the real elephants, because the real elephants are a natural expression of themselves.

If you pretend to be something you are not, the power to invent your future will elude you. Question your true nature and purpose. Discover and integrate the lessons in your life that are pointing to your calling. When you're "in the zone," like a world-class athlete, you can perform according to your deepest nature without even thinking about it. These moments give you a glimpse into your true self. I have discovered this, and I am integrating my natural gifts into my life. My purpose is to help others do the same.

If you do not start from your true nature, no roadmap will help you invent your future. Your future emerges, and is manifest, in the present. It is your destiny—a strong and deep current in the flow of your life, yet often you may not feel its pull. (Many of us float along its edges, confused about who we are, like a dying fish caught in an eddy behind a fallen log.) Only when you know who you are at the deepest level will you be able to master swimming in your destiny's current. Once you know who you are, mastery begins. The first step is always learning who you are meant to be. In this book you will learn who you are meant to be.

Discover the Answer

Once you know your natural genius and calling, with practice you can learn to see the future emerge from the present. You can feel and see the currents turn in your bones. You can more easily know the right answer. Most important, you have to know when you know so that you can act at the right moment, like a basketball player driving to the basket, "in the zone." It is not enough to say, after it is too late, "I knew that."

In any endeavor, opportunities open and close. When you are energized by your destiny's current, you see the opening as it first begins to emerge and can gracefully leap through it.

Paint Compelling Pictures

Sailors pick a landmark or a star in the night sky to keep them on course. They sail into the sunset if they are going west, or away from the evening sun if they are going east. Creating a clear, compelling picture of your future state is key. You cannot create something you cannot conceive.

Once you know the answer, or the right course, you must be able to conceive and communicate your opportunities, first as a guide to yourself, and then to those who might help you. No one has ever succeeded without help. Until the people in your world can see, feel, and hear the calling of your opportunity that present reality represents, they cannot truly help you, nor can you help yourself.

With this book you will learn how to create simple, compelling pictures that attract people who naturally share a common mission and destiny with you. You also will learn how to create a vortex of actions that leads to mutual success.

Build Commitment

After you can see and feel the possibility of the future, your commitment will be able to grow and root in your heart, and your clear-eyed passion will radiate out to others. Still, when the journey seems long and goals far away, commitment often weakens. Goethe, the German poet, playwright, novelist, philosopher, and scientist, said:

> *"Until one is committed, there is hesitancy, the chance to draw back. Concerning all acts of initiative (and creation), there is one elementary truth that ignorance of which kills countless ideas and splendid plans: that the moment one definitely commits oneself, then Providence moves too. All sorts of things occur to help one that would never otherwise have occurred. A whole stream of events issues from the decision, raising in one's favor all manner of unforeseen incidents and meetings and material assistance, which no man could have dreamed would have come his way. Whatever you can do, or dream you can do, begin it. Boldness has genius, power, and magic in it. Begin it now."*

First, you must be fully committed to the mission and then inspire the same level of commitment in those who follow or support you in life. We all become committed and then fall back. To invent our futures, we must continuously recommit ourselves and those who would walk with us. They need to feel the draw of your mission, and see progress each day.

With this book, you will learn how to master building commitment in yourself, others, and in the world at large.

Respond to Reality

When I have fallen short of my goals, I have often skipped or distorted this step—to respond to reality. No matter how committed you may be to a mission, having the wrong starting point can make your plans useless. Knowing the good, the bad, and the ugly about any situation you face enables you to respond in a manner that is targeted and effective. Often we believe what we want to believe to protect our egos from being wrong. By doing this, we distort reality, thinking we are in one place when actually we are in another.

The flow of cause and effect is multidimensional, ever changing, and has a momentum. To influence this momentum, I have found that I have to dance with its ebb and flow, and then create a new direction within that rhythm and flow.

With this book you will learn how to respond to the flow of reality effortlessly.

Master Inner Stillness

In martial arts, it is said that a master can tell who will win a match as the competitors bow to each other before it even begins. The master knows that the one who has the most stillness, or presence, will come out on top. Like a powerful hurricane, there is stillness at the center of power. It is the way of nature.

Stillness lets you see present reality and respond accurately, instead of distorting reality with your thoughts. Throughout this book I offer practices that will build conscious connection to your inner stillness. As you understand these practices and how to apply them in your life, we will work on synchronizing all of them together.

Minimize Psychological Filtering

As leaders of organizations, communities, or families and friends, the most powerful tool we have is an accurate view of present reality. Our ego tends to distort our perception. Once we decide we want something or have the correct view about a person or organization, our ego looks for proof instead of looking at present reality. For example, once I started thinking about buying a Cadillac CTS, I noticed more of them on the road. If I develop a prejudice about a person or race, looking through my ego, I look for proof. If I have an inflated or deflated view of myself, I will not be able to accurately invent my future. The starting point will be wrong. If I am fearful or depressed, I am likely to miss opportunities, hesitating to take risks. Mastering inner stillness takes practice but is the best cure.

Fears Tend to Dominate Consciousness

"We are born to manifest the glory of God within us."
—**Mary Ann Williamson**

But what happens to those who do? Jesus was crucified and tortured, and many people who we now recognize as geniuses were persecuted in their day. Nelson Mandela, who used this quotation in his first speech as president of South Africa after twenty-five years in prison knew, yet transcended, this fear. Many entrepreneurs have failed many times, and have been persecuted in various ways, but have still gotten up and succeeded. In fact, to get funding in the San Francisco Bay Area, some say that you have to have failed at least once. Investors want to know you have learned from your mistakes.

PRACTICES and ACTIONS

As I often stated in my previous book, *Unleashing Genius*, there is no substitute for practice. Please be sure to follow the Practices and Actions provided at the end of each chapter. Work with them until you reach a comfortable level of mastery and then move on to the next chapter. Each set of practices builds on the others, and usually includes the following:

1. A clear description of why the practice is important to inventing your future.
2. Quotations from successful leaders.
3. How to adapt what these leaders have learned to your life.
4. Exercises you can use to build your future.
5. Links to videos and articles that support your journey, found at www. inventyourfuturebook.com.
6. Links to the Facebook page called *Invent Your Future*, where you can ask me questions and share your insights and successes with others.

Jump into this book and integrate its lessons into your life. Do not read this book to know the answers, but read it to begin a practice that will change your life, and that of your family. Pass these skills down to your children, and those who might be on your business team. It is the only true choice.

How to Invent Your Future

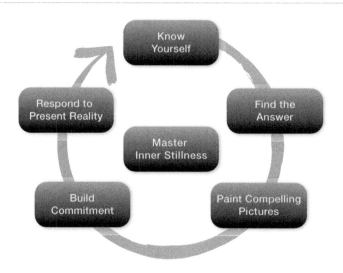

Wisdom from Successful Leaders

One of the most difficult jobs in the world is to lead complex organizations. The women and men who occupy the top executive positions in these companies are always tasked with inventing their futures. Once you are at the top of any organization, no one but you can be accountable for this process and its ultimate outcome. This same dynamic is true for all of us as we shape our own lives and careers.

This prologue showcases the success philosophies of the many successful leaders who have invented their own futures, and have contributed their wisdom to this book. Their observations are presented in full here, and then are excerpted in the context of the following chapters. Wisdom often comes from moments of stillness. While you read this book, take time to reflect in beautiful environments that lift your spirits.

Photo: Sarah Clarehart

There is much wisdom to be found in the thoughts and philosophies of those who have attained success. That's why, especially for this book, I interviewed leaders from various industries to discover how they successfully invented the future for themselves and their businesses. Their perceptions are featured throughout, in their own words.

Read these stories carefully. Understand that none of these individuals were handed their current organizations and titles. They invented them using their natural genius. I have strived to add context to their statements, and I am sharing these thoughts in a way that will empower you to use their empowering practices to achieve success in your own life.

Read through these stories and make notes in your journal. Write down any insight you have, no matter how incomplete or insignificant. When you finish, you will notice patterns that may help you.

This is just the beginning. Subsequent chapters delve deeper into every facet of inventing the future, and will excerpt many of the quotations you'll first see here.

Photo courtesy of G.J. Hart

G. J. HART: *Chairman and Chief Executive Officer, California Pizza Kitchen*

We all face obstacles to inventing our future. G.J. Hart had many, yet he faced them and not only succeeded, but did so with compassion and humility. Listen to him talk to the press.

G.J.'s family came to America from the Netherlands when he was five years old, and he had to work that much harder in any situation to be a normal kid. He had to learn English. He went to an affluent high school where the other children's parents were doctors and lawyers, but he was a cop's kid.

He found a job at a poultry processing plant during college, and worked his way up. He became general manager of the plant when he was 21, overseeing 500 people. He had done pretty much every role in the operation. That was a big advantage—gaining first-hand experience in what his people did every day. That helped him understand his employees and help them grow.

Before joining California Pizza Kitchen, G.J. was CEO of Texas Roadhouse, which owns, operates, and franchises more than 350 restaurants. During his ten years there, he led the company through an unprecedented period of growth, increasing revenues from $63 million to more than $1 billion.

G.J. invested in California Pizza Kitchen (CPK) with the commitment to bring this classic brand back to prominence, and also established a number of funds to help those in need. The company's annual awards banquet became a stage to talk about helping the communities CPK serves. Vendors and their spouses, along with CPK general managers, executives, and their spouses (600 people) went out into the town, which has no CPKs anywhere nearby, in teams to help most of the nonprofits.

Here's what G.J. has to say about leadership:

> *Leadership is about getting people to exceed their own expectations. You can't do that unless you understand what they do and how they do it, having lived some of it yourself.*

> *I've always wanted to make a difference in people's lives and in an organization. It is not about me, it is about how I serve others.*

> *Courage is an interesting concept because any leadership role is about stepping out and having the courage to be different, because you have to be different to be a leader.*

> *Be the very best that you can be, because you can't lead anybody if you can't lead yourself. So you have to be honest with yourself about your good qualities, your bad qualities, and the things you need to work on.*

Dream big. What's the world of possibilities for yourself and for your organization? You have to be able to say, "Here's where I want to go." It's not that you'll ever necessarily get there, but if you don't dream, you'll never even get started.

Lead with your heart first. Let people see that you're human. Show people that you have compassion. It doesn't mean that you don't set expectations and standards. But if you lead with your heart, people will figure out whether you're genuine, whether you're real.

The hardest thing for young leaders is to trust the people they lead. It's about letting go, and allowing people to grow into leadership roles. At the end of the day, it's okay if they make a mistake or if they fall down. Because, as leaders, it's your job to pick them back up.

If you genuinely believe in that person, sometimes it takes courage to do the right thing and offer a second chance. That's because we've all made mistakes and somebody picked us up.

It's ultimately about serving the people you lead. It's about putting the cause before yourself, and being willing to see it through. I developed a list of imperatives over time because it's the way I live each day. My job is to lead and to make a difference. I'm a catalyst for change, to create an environment where people can grow and prosper.

We're most imaginative when we're being ourselves. We want our guests and our people to share their personalities, expertise, and passion for food—and embrace their diversity of backgrounds and tastes.

Photo courtesy of David LeFevre

DAVID LeFEVRE, *Chef and Owner, Manhattan Beach Post and Fishing with Dynamite*

David LeFevre nearly missed pursuing his dream, but something inside told him not to give up. He listened and had the courage to act.

David grew up in Wisconsin. Because he was very good at math, science, and music, his guidance counselor suggested he get an engineering degree. So, he went to college. After a short time he remembered his dream in middle school about being a chef, way before doing that was cool. He used to watch his mother make biscuits, which are now on his menus.

David left college, enrolled in the Culinary Institute of America, and worked with some of the world's greatest chefs. About three and one half years ago, opened his first restaurant, Manhattan Beach Post. He invested his life savings, designed the food, the interior, and the music playlist, and opened with a great success. He paid off his investors in a little over two years, and opened a new restaurant, Fishing with Dynamite, which is also successful. Of these two successes, Manhattan Beach Post has been listed as one of the top restaurants in the United States by *The Los Angeles Times*, and suggested as a destination for dinner in the *The New York Times*.

Here are some valuable thoughts on success from David:

> *I knew in middle school that I wanted to learn how to cook from my mother. I knew I enjoyed doing it. I did not know anything about how to do it. I just knew the result.*

> *I spent basically all of my twenties and thirties trying to surround myself with the best culinary minds in the world, and even with that determination the recipe that I got from my mother is the one that everyone freaks out about.*

> *I looked up culinary schools in a guide, and the one that had four pages dedicated to it was the Culinary Institute of America. It was the best, and I decided at twenty years old to enroll.*

> *The culinary school work was easy for me because I combined my high level of pattern recognition with my love for cooking.*

> *I was pretty nervous opening Post. I didn't know if it was going to work. And I had put basically all of my life savings into it.*

> *I put together six storyboards and a soundtrack to communicate my vision to the architects—the type of ethos my guests would want. I surrounded myself with great people in the industry.*

I remember the day the restaurant took shape. I had this vision for the way it should look and feel. I went outside for five minutes, and when I returned, the Ramones were playing, the dining room was set, the crew was ready and I saw it all come together. I knew in that moment it was going to be a success.

I am a very self-reflective guy.

Pattern recognition is important to being a chef. You analyze a process to figure out when it has gone right and wrong. What you do all day is think for other people. I am always looking for a better way.

I wanted to open something I would enjoy doing for ten to twenty years; something I would have fun with and someday give away; something that keeps me and the public happy.

It is a very blue-collar job. I want to teach and mentor my team to give them a chance at the American Dream.

If you can make the lives of the people around you better, you make your life better. That is what we teach. The dollars come from that ideal, not from wanting the dollars.

I had to work on my vision, and learned how to coach people toward integrity, humility, and respect ... you can solve any problem inside that circle.

I have several mentors in my life who can advise and coach me.

I give feedback and coaching not to be the bad guy, but to live my commitment to developing the wellbeing of my crew.

We are not the best, but we will always be better than we were yesterday.

My biggest challenge was the transition from being a great cook to teaching and leading. At this point I am learning to lead and teach. I practice being a good leader every day.

CASEY SHEAHAN: *Former Chief Executive Officer, Patagonia, Inc.*

Casey Sheahan always loved the outdoors, and built a career that is all about his love. He leads a company that gives all its profits to environmental causes. His career and passion are one. Take a look at this video where Casey talks about conscious leadership.

Photo courtesy of Casey Sheahan

After Casey launched the Patagonia Footprint Chronicles, which displays the company's carbon footprint for all products on their website, I told him that I thought that the concept was genius. He responded, "When I look back on that decision, the fact that it was smart looks more like 'that guy was just a master of the obvious,' and it seems simple when you actually see what the outcome and the strategy is now. It's like 'wow, that was dumb' ... it was right here under our noses."

Here are some other thoughts from Casey:

> We launched Footprint Chronicles with five apparel styles, and we got a huge amount of attention. We got attention on the blogosphere, we got emails from our customers, and we received letters addressed to Yvon Chouinard [the founder of Patagonia] and me. What surprised me was we actually got a lot of input from scientists, researchers, academics, and customers about ways in which we could actually further improve how we were producing our garments globally, and how we can reduce our footprint even more.

> This not only created this extreme transparency around how we were operating the company, but it brought in a global perspective on how we can further minimize our impact. That was unexpected, but a really wonderful added benefit, and I feel like it's a lesson. The truth will often set you free, and when you are in a leadership position of a company, my take is that you are customer-based and the whole world is watching you whether it's the media or whoever. They are really not interested in half-truths.

> Be calm and centered before you make decisions.

When you get older, service becomes an important aspect of what everybody does.

A practice of mindfulness and commitment to the community, a dedication to innovation and compassion, are an important part of what we do. Patagonia is a caring company.

I think it is important to raise your own level of consciousness before others can shift along with you, whether as an individual leader or as a company.

Mindfulness and presence fosters a lot of creativity.

Being aware, acknowledging and responding to your present reality is critical. Because if you don't understand the problems you have, or the problems you are creating, you won't be able to find solutions to them.

Patagonia's sales grew 20 percent to 30 percent a year, through the recession.

There's no global transformation possible without personal transformation. The founder of Patagonia led the way by evoking Gandhi's words, "We have to live simply so others may simply live."

I feel very positive that the future is bright, am a positive person in general, but I think that an example like Patagonia being able to have an impact that is much larger than the company is important. This success has given me a lot of hope that there is a new paradigm that is emerging that will be very positive for society in general, and for the environment. This is important in that we have to sustain six to seven billion people on the planet.

The vision and values set by Yvon Chouinard thirty-five to forty years ago have moved the company along in positive ways, and was the result of a number of transformative moments … moving to organic cotton or getting rid of unnecessary packaging, and making fleece jackets out of soda pop bottles instead of raw materials.

All those were environmental moments that came because he saw what could happen when he looked over the horizon, realizing that if we didn't alter our way of doing business, we would all be in trouble.

Slow down, take care of yourself. If we all listened to our internal guide, we would find it's always for the best. We just have to be willing to listen to our own wisdom, our truest self.

When I am "in the zone" in work or play, which is really the same at Patagonia, it feels effortless.

Work and life should be a lot of fun. A lot of people look at Patagonia and say, "Guys, everything seems so easy for you!" And it's true. We are being tremendously successful right now, and we are having a lot of fun. We like what we are doing; we like the impact we are having; we like that the success is feeding itself.

Inspiration has to start with you. If you don't believe that you can affect positive change, then it won't happen. But if you can inspire people, as opposed to motivating them with fear, then you know there is a better outcome possible, and the company will come along with you.

I think you can really light people up. You can light your customers up, and you can light your manufacturers up too. When people are inspired, you get a better result, working conditions, and high-quality products. It is a priority for us.

I think that what's been proven in the recent global economic crisis is that operating from a place of fear has been completely useless to leadership.

Being "in the zone" is when you are operating as your authentic self in the work you are doing.

The companies that are succeeding right now have leaders who have a personal practice of mindfulness and centeredness, using exercise, meditation, or yoga. These practices are quite helpful. They help leaders come into the workplace and exude a certain calm, peace, centeredness, balance, and confidence. I learned a lot of these from athletics, in sports such as surfing, cycling, and fly fishing. When you get into a zone, a tremendous power and confidence fills your being.

Photo courtesy of Stanton Rowe

STANTON J. ROWE: *Corporate Vice President, Advanced Technology and Chief Scientific Officer, Edwards Lifesciences*

Stanton Rowe and his team invented a device that can replace your heart valve without open heart surgery. Doctors and the medical industry did not believe it to be possible. Their first patient, mortally ill, was in France. During the procedure the patient went into cardiac arrest, but the doctors inserted the new heart valve anyway, and he came back to life. Hours afterward, he sat up and started talking. It was a front-page headline in Paris, ahead of a major election result. Stanton's belief in this process drove him to success. He sold his company to Edwards Lifesciences for a lot of money, and he has saved many lives.

Here is what Stanton told me when I asked him what it takes to invent your future:

> It takes a lot of hard work and practice.
>
> You have to look at the world a little differently.
>
> Ask the stupid questions … Why would I send a nonsurgical patient to a surgeon?
>
> I have been turned down by all of the top venture capitalists on Silicon Valley's Sand Hill Road
>
> Don't judge too quickly.
>
> You have to be a good sales person; accept rejection, but never give up.
>
> You have to be a strategist. You have to plan for your success and commit to it up front. For example, we bought a key patent ($3 million + 3.5 percent equity) before we made it work. We believed and took the risk. The patent would have cost much more if the sellers knew it would work.

Diversity matters … Don't hire people just like you.

Seek perfection; plan, execute, modify, and make it work.

First, you have to figure out what does not work.

The best argument wins in an optimal culture for innovation.

Look inside yourself and your company … what am I good at and what am I not good at?

We failed a lot—95 percent of the time.

Customers do not know what they want until you hand it to them.

When someone does not believe you, you have to listen, but you may still be right; radical innovation is not accepted by the status quo.

LINDA LoRe: *Chief Executive Officer, Frederick's of Hollywood*

Linda LoRe came from Giorgio Beverly Hills to a broken and sad organizational culture at Frederick's of Hollywood. "There were 1,800 employees and they were good people. They had talents. They had skills, but they were very broken-spirited," she has noted.

Photo courtesy of Linda LoRe

She had seen the direct opposite at Giorgio Beverly Hills, where she was CEO. This experience gave her confidence, and a knowing about the possibility of something better.

Here are several choice observations from Linda:

There was something inside me because I had just come from an organization that worked. It flew so high and so fast, and it was a wonderful experience with Giorgio Beverly Hills. It just grew and, wow, I loved it. It was so exciting. I thought I had to bring just a portion of that excitement and enthusiasm, combined in a cohesiveness that is in Giorgio Beverly Hills. I said to myself, "I'll try to capture that capability in this new organization to help people. And if I can do that, it will really be an exciting thing."

A big portion of excitement and enthusiasm comes from leadership. It is about understanding where one is going.

I never paid attention to the naysayers. I mean, I heard what they were saying, I noticed it, but I didn't let that get in my way, because fear is the most crippling emotion that an organization can have, or a person can have.

I truly believe our thoughts are very powerful. They are so powerful that they can change what ultimately can become our destiny.

What I have been able to do is to separate the naysayers, and say, okay, I'm going to prove them wrong; or, okay, I hear what they are saying, and I will validate. If there is something valid that comes out of them, I will use that for my benefit. Because, generally speaking, naysayers are just afraid.

As an example of total commitment, here is what happened when Linda saved the company, which seemed impossible, by applying for bankruptcy protection.

We had to petition the court for cash collateral and the ability to reorganize. This was a big risk, because once you file, then you will have a hearing. When the hearing happens, it's in the judge's hands whether or not he'll grant you the ability to reorganize, or whether he'll just order liquidation.

So here's what happened. I called each of the vendors, and I said, "If you will write a letter stating that you want us to have the ability to reorganize, and that you will grant us terms, in other words you will grant us credit, we will have a chance with the court."

I walked into that courtroom with twenty-six letters in my hand. That had never been done before, because companies just don't come out very well in Chapter 11. There were three chairs on the witness stand. I was white-knuckling it the whole way, and I knew the bank would say, "Frederick's owes us that money."

Once they called our company an institution, it gave us a shot at reorganizing.

First we presented the vendor letters. There were 1,800 families who would be out of work, many of whom were there, and about twenty-five companies that would be severely hurt.

Linda won the case, and ultimately saved Frederick's of Hollywood through pure commitment. She carried what she knew was possible from her work with Giorgio Beverly Hills in her heart, and it all worked together.

BILL McGINNIS: *Chief Executive Officer, NTS Corporation*

Bill McGinnis worked for National Technical Systems (NTS) for twenty-five years. He started as an entry-level employee, and over time became the CEO. He is a Boston-born man who loves to tell stories and laugh. One member of his team said, "You can hear him before you see him."

Photo courtesy of Bill McGinnis

Bill's challenge was to change a company that he had been part of for most of his career. As they say, "It is hard to be a prophet in your own land," but Bill became that prophet.

Here is the story Bill told me when I asked him how he had invented his and his company's future.

I knew that if we didn't do something different, our company would continue down the same path and get the same results. Frankly, we were going backwards. Even though we did not know what to do, our level of knowing that we were on the wrong path, which is often hard to face, opened us to new possibilities.

Probably the hardest thing for me was to recognize who I was. Once I knew my natural gifts, I started painting the picture of my future. It was the same for our company. We didn't quite know what we needed to do differently, but we knew we had to do something. That in itself was a breakthrough. At that point we already had a clear and compelling picture of what would not work.

Did I know six years ago at a meeting in Boston [with NTS's Board of Directors] what the picture should look like? The answer was "no." But I could not tell them we were working closely with our senior staff, and collectively we painted the picture that we could all get behind and live with. And that's where I think the alignment came.

What I had to do at that point with my senior executives was not only to paint the picture of what we could create, but what was in it for them. I had to convince them they were going to be safe; basically, not losing their current roles.

Having the team involved in painting the picture was directly related to their level of commitment. I could have painted the correct picture myself, but then it would be just my picture. I am sure it would have taken a lot longer than it finally did, due to resistance and fear, and it would have been a lot more challenging. The change we had to make might never have happened.

So having my team be part of painting that picture, rather than simply giving them targets, is why it became so compelling to them and the market. Once they knew what they needed to do, and what was in it for them, they started executing with a velocity that was amazing. When we got that committed, we thought we could do anything. It's crazy. We actually did. We actually went from a company that was going backwards, certainly retracting, to a company that turned around to be, in our space, one of the fastest growing firms compared to our competitors.

The clarity we shared allowed flexibility and experimentation as unforeseen challenges arose. We moved like a team "in the zone" and found a new path to the picture we all could see. Had we not come together, we could have actually taken our company slowly down the wrong path, and the turnaround may not have worked.

It is important to know that during the process you don't have to be a hundred percent right. When we're not, let's adjust; let's change; let's talk about it; let's figure it out. If we still haven't figured it out, let's start again.

Working with openness, flexibility, and commitment to each other is the key. I would say that honest discussions with a true level of caring for one another allows you to make the changes needed to invent your future.

I fundamentally believe that people, given the opportunity, want to be incredibly successful. So, I create an environment that enables them to succeed. I think that's where that inner stillness thrives. Everyone is committed to each other's success and feels safe. There is very little fear or backbiting—just the harmony of our voices. When you recognize people for their true talent and beauty, and help them recognize themselves for their true genius, you empower them.

All of those big life-changing decisions, and not-so-life-changing decisions, whether it's a house or a career change, go best when we are really honest with ourselves. Know yourself, and know when you know, and then act with power and clarity. It's really important to know yourself, and what you really want to do, and then you'll know if you're ready to go forward with vigor.

Why are you changing your career? Are you running away from something? If you really take a look at yourself, you could be incredibly successful. That's why, when you're responding to reality, presence is so important, because you can't be over here in your picture. You've got to be present to what's going on now. But you carry that intention, and you make it happen, one way or the other.

When things go wrong, I think those are your best opportunities for growth. But certainly, if you create an environment where people feel threatened, you will never have a high-performance team, nor will you achieve your dreams without the help of others. Of that I am certain.

Photo courtesy of Tim Pulido

TIM PULIDO: *President and Chief Executive Officer, Campero USA and Pollo Campero International*

Tim Pulido is a leader who stays close to his team. He speaks Spanish and makes a point of going back into the kitchen and talking with the cooks and dishwashers. After turning around Shakey's Pizza, he now leads a Guatemalan restaurant brand, Pollo Campero, that is expanding into North America.

When I asked Tim to describe how he invents the future, he told me this story:

> *I came in as president of Shakey's Pizza. This was a brand that had been at one time a leader of its category years and years ago, but now had declining sales for well over a decade. It was one of those brands that looked like it was rolling into the morgue. First I met with my team, and we went out and looked at the competition. Everyone looked at the products, looked at the experience of the competitors. Then we met back at Shakey's, and we said, "All right, here is the Shakey's experience; how does it compare with the competition?"*

> *We talked about how our stores were very old and tired, that we looked like a 1950s or 1960s brand, and that our product quality had degraded. We were using the same skim milk–quality cheese on top that other people were. We weren't leveraging our heritage or point of difference. We were just like an old brand. We still had some guests who remembered it fondly as a kid, but today it was not good.*

> *Yet, since it was not the executive team's idea, I had a hard time convincing them, even in the face of a consumer revolt, that we needed to change direction. I had to get the team to recognize that we had made strategic errors. No one wanted to admit that we had drifted from our roots. So we went back to the consumer—and this is also a critical principle of creating a compelling story or a compelling picture.*

I really feel that when, as a leader, you simply declare that something is important, it has a lot less legitimacy than when you say, "We've gone back to our customers, our guests, and they have told us the following ..." The latter approach puts you on higher ground to create a more powerful and compelling picture. So, we went back to our consumers, and they told us the issues they had with this new product, and more importantly they started giving us insight.

After viewing the competition, we took the best of their innovations and built model stores to test our ideas. We created a living vision of our ideas. When we combined all of those things—uniforms, products, remodeled stores, improved games, and everything else—suddenly the total package came together. Our restaurants were seeing 15 to 20 percent growth.

I use what I call the four Cs: clarity, commitment, courage, and character. Clarity is my way of acknowledging reality with brutal facts. As you confront those, they lead you to what you need to do in any situation. When you can look at them objectively, they lead you to knowing the answer to any problem or strategy. Clarity for me is what I call strategic clarity or business clarity—you know clearly what you want to be, and how you are going to get there. As Paul says, the compelling picture is then in place.

Your commitment to cleaning up everything that does not support that compelling picture is important. When you have it right, and know it, you want new principles, and a different level of commitment. You clean out the old and bring in the new, but often people have difficulty letting go of the old. It takes a high level of commitment.

That is where the third C, courage, comes into play. Even though the living vision of our model stores indicated the formula for success, people at all levels in the organization needed the courage to change behaviors that they had gotten used to. It takes courage to let go of something you know and try something new. Essentially, you have to admit you were wrong, and then you have to go through the clumsy period of trying new ways. Then you have to polish your act.

My fourth C is character, which is, you can argue, part of clarity. Clarity supports your commitment and gives you courage, but you have to be in a position where you walk the talk. People have to get a sense that you know the right course as leader. You must display an inner strength. This inner strength leads to accomplishment. People feel you will make the right call in most situations. With all of this in place, you know your calling. So … clarity, commitment, courage, and character: that's going to be my opening talk to my new executive team this coming Monday.

Photo courtesy of Tony LoRe

TONY LoRe: *Founder and Chief Executive Officer, Youth Mentoring Connection*

Tony LoRe (yes, he is Linda's brother) was an Orange County, California businessman. He was invited to an entrepreneurism program for youth in South Central Los Angeles. Coming from an upper-middle-class neighborhood, he drove to the event, just blocks from the inner-city corner of Florence and Normandie made famous for the violent uprising in the 1970s riots. He was already feeling out of his element when he pulled into an alley to find parking at the facility, and a gang's activities blocked his entrance. Something told him that he had better not get out of the car and ask them to move. So he just sat in his vehicle reading and doing other things, being careful not to stare at them, and acting as if this was just a normal stop on the road. After a short time, which seemed like forever, the gang moved on, and he pulled into the facility.

Once inside, he witnessed a teacher working with teens from that area, many of them in gangs. After watching how the teacher engaged these kids, Tony jumped in. He was amazed at his ability to connect with these youth, who seemed to come from a totally different world. He had always been good with kids, but never realized that this gift would translate so well across cultural and ethnic boundaries. At that moment, he realized he had found his calling.

He sold his business and started the Youth Mentoring Connection in 2000. Though it was a constant struggle to find funds, Tony says he has never looked back. "What would you give to know why you were put on this planet?" he asks. Despite the challenges associated with the toughest teens in one of the most violent neighborhoods in the country, 96 percent of Tony's youth graduate high school, and the majority of those go on to college.

Here is what Tony told me when I asked him what it takes to help these teens invent a future for themselves:

What I have discovered is that a person's gift sits right next to his or her wounds. If you don't shy away from dealing with that "woundedness," that person's gift (which has been wanting to come out all along) will become evident. Some believe that your gift first shows up when you are eight or nine years old. How the family or community responds to it will determine whether you are going to protect yourself by hiding it away, or expand and live into it.

Here is a famous story about Showtime at the Apollo on amateur night. The announcer up on stage says, "Our next performer is an eight-year-old young lady who is going to dance for us." Then this little kid comes running across the stage, and whispers in the announcer's ears. "Oh ... correction, she's decided that she's gonna sing, so everybody welcome Miss Ella Fitzgerald." Her gift was displayed in front of the crowd. She stood in amazement as the applause rang out. Her gift was recognized and she got to live fully into it.

A true visionary is the one who can hold a vision when everybody else is giving up on it. We are all brought into this life with a noble, beautiful purpose. We are here for a reason. We each have a gift, and it is our job to find it. This is why we don't tell kids to change. In fact, I correct them when they say, "I'm gonna change." I say, "I don't want you to change, I want you to become more of who you are."

This translates to my staff as well. The first question I ask anyone wanting to get involved with Youth Mentoring Connection is, "What's your vision for your life?" It thrills most people, even though they do not know how to answer. So immediately we take what we do with our kids and practice it with our employees, our staff, and our board members.

It takes a monumental amount of effort to run this organization. People ask me why I don't burn out, and they warn me that I am going to burn out. My answer is always, "I don't believe I can burn out if am always in my purpose." If I stray from my purpose or calling, I don't get the energy. My vision, my reason for being, my passion, gives me all the energy I need.

Photo courtesy of Kristen Allison

KRISTEN ALLISON: *Chief Executive Officer, Burnham Benefits*

Kristen Allison's company was ranked "#1 Best Place To Work" by *Business Insurance Magazine* in Orange County, California, with strong financial results as well. Burnham has cultivated all the services you would expect from the nation's largest benefits consulting firms, and they bring them to small and mid-sized employers who demand the best from their consulting partners.

When I asked Kristen to tell me about one of her secrets to success, she said this:

I don't take things personally, because it is not about me. It is about everybody. I do not want to be the center of attention. I just want to be proud of the place.

I just say I had a great dad who treated everybody with respect. He really had employees to the dinner table, and he treated them well. They protected him and gave back what they got, and his business was a success. That concept is basically so simple.

We are all in this together. I just want to be proud of the place where we work. I want everyone to be respected and trusted, and do a great job. I know that stress damages people and their performance, so I do everything to eliminate stress. I want people to have a nice, quality life. I try to build a drama-free zone.

TOM DAVIN: *Chief Executive Officer, 511 Tactical*

Tom Davin, CEO of 511 Tactical, is a living example of aligning his work with his natural gifts and passion. Tom is a graduate from the Marine Officer Basic School, the U.S. Army Ranger School, and the Special Forces Combat Diver Course. He holds an AB degree from Duke University and an MBA from Harvard Business

Photo courtesy of Tom Davin

School. And, as you may know, once a Marine, always a Marine.

Tom has often used his leadership skills for his board positions, and has been CEO and president of Panda Restaurant Group, Inc. He also has served as an operating partner of Brentwood Associates and many other firms. 511 Tactical makes clothing and gear for first responders of all kinds. His team is made up of ex-military, police, and SWAT team people. His term for corporate culture is "ethos."

I recently toured the company's new facility, where we went through a training space filled with equipment. As he showed me a rope strung from the ceiling, he climbed to the top to illustrate the shoes he was wearing. He is a living example of the company's vision.

Here is how Tom defines his "ethos":

> Our vision for the clothing and gear we offer is: "For those who train with a higher purpose." A picture here is worth a thousand words.

Photo courtesy of Tom Davin

He then told me a story about a young Marine officer, Travis Manion, who had been killed in Iraq.

> *In April 2014, to honor Travis Manion, a man who gave his life for our country, some friends and a Marine buddy who was with him when he died came to do a series of CrossFit workouts of the day ("WODs"). We wrote Travis's name on the wall, along with numbers representing how many reps the group would do of each exercise to honor him. Those numbers represented the date he was killed, consisting of seven rounds (representing 2007, the year he died) of 400-meter runs (for the fourth month of the year) and nineteen back squats (representing the day). Before we began, Travis's buddy told a story about him and had to go down on one knee. There was not a dry eye in the house. Of course, next we all suffered through the workout together.*

> *We invite top trainers to come in and train our employees each week, and people can train at any time. We have men's and women's showers, so it's easy for everyone to find time to make fitness part of their daily routine.*

> *Accountability is key here. We seek to achieve results with a bias for action. We like to compete and be measured against the most demanding standards to ensure our continued success.*

> *At 511 Tactical, our mission is to be an innovator that creates purpose-built gear for the most demanding missions. We strive to create trust in everything we do. That starts with self trust and relationship trust. We work on the components of integrity, intent, capability, and results.*

> *We listen to the needs of our end-user professionals, and then develop, produce, and deliver solutions to their problems. Each of us chooses to be a leader and take charge of what is within our circle of influence.*

> *We overcome obstacles to accomplish our goals and support our team members when challenges arise. We complete commitments and seek to "over deliver" relative to expectations.*

Most of what Tom had told me was in a flyer that he sent to me later. Tom is a perfect example of someone who knows himself, and leads a business around his passion. A mutual friend sent him an email suggesting he was at the peak of his life, and he replied, "No, I am just getting started!"

LAWRENCE KOH: *President, International Diversified Products*

Lawrence Koh started his business career as a gang leader dealing drugs. Through work with organizations such as the University of Santa Monica, he transformed himself, and leads a company that invents and produces products and technologies that make a difference in people's lives.

Photo courtesy of Lawrence Koh

He is one of the most gentle and present leaders I have ever met. International Diversified Products has a design and sales office in Los Angeles, and nearly three thousand employees in China.

Here are some of the things Lawrence said to me, and a link to a video.

We cultivate our employees instead of trying to change them.

When something resonates to our purpose in life, when something resonates to a contribution that we want to make, when something resonates to a service that we want to perform, there is a solidity and a recognition that takes place within you. When you follow this resonance, this inner guidance, this experience, it becomes easier for you to recognize over time.

When this resonance is present, it does not matter whether it involves a product, a technology, or a service. The emergence of your purpose, your inner calling, will begin coloring your life with a mystical quality and a depth of meaning that far exceeds the goal of making a profit.

Life is more rewarding, fulfilling, and complete when we align to that. These are things that when they appear they usually cause us to say, "Wow, this is a great idea" (versus a good idea), meaning that though it emerged from within us, it was given to us. When we recognize the spiritual quality of this action, we become profoundly impacted by it.

So if I sit around and think of ways to make money, that is likely going to be very difficult. But if I am looking for something that inspires me, that resonates to my purpose, that gives meaning to my life and enables me to contribute through serving, then a huge bed of ideas will begin to surface in my awareness, and opportunities related to these ideas will begin to present themselves.

Consider the relationship between tuning forks in different notes. If you hit a tuning fork tuned to a C note, and place another tuning fork tuned to the same key next to it, it will begin to resonate or vibrate, even if they're tuned to different octaves. However, if you place it next to a tuning fork tuned to any other note, they will not resonate. Physics has proven that everything in life carries with it a specific particular. In other words, everything has a specific vibratory aspect and, like the tuning forks, this is how "like attracts like" in life.

This resonance with my purpose or calling rings out authentically in my life and engulfs everyone around me. When I am living my purpose it enables me to be patient and humble with clients and members of my team. The resonance that my purpose or calling carries does much of the work when I allow it to do so.

For example, I was trying to close a big account, and kept calling this potential client over the course of a year and a half. I did so because I felt that what we offered resonated with his company's purpose and their market. But initially, he was unable to see that. So without judgment or anger, I would call, talk to his assistant, and leave a message with her. Over that year and a half, I developed a good relationship with his assistant, never complaining about how many times I was required to call and never making her boss wrong. I simply explained that it was my responsibility to our firm and to his company that, at the very least, I explain the significant contribution our firm could make to his. Finally, he invited me to meet with him to discuss the project. I believe that the alignment of my purpose to his company's purpose helped him to connect to the resonance of the calling within me. The meeting went very well, and our companies are currently doing business together.

HENRY WALKER: *President, Farmers and Merchants Bank*

Henry Walker is the fourth generation of Walkers (we are not related) to be CEO of Farmers and Merchants Bank, which was rated during the financial crisis as one of the strongest midsized banks in California. Few family businesses survive the third generation. When I asked him why this was, he said:

Photo courtesy of Henry Walker

In our family, every member has to carry his or her weight. No one gets a free ride. We have always earned our way into positions in the bank and elsewhere. We put a high value on total accountability, and we each do what we are best suited for.

Our brand of quality and service is important to us. We make sure every manager and employee not only understands our vision, but also knows exactly how we expect it to be implemented through financial strength and service.

Each person in the company understands that we expect the following behaviors, which we feel are important to our success.

- *Smile—we want to create a friendly environment in our banks.*
- *Get to know customers by name and understand what their lives are about.*
- *Cross-sell the bank's different products to meet the needs of their lives.*

To be sure that our employees are committed and stay committed, I have people "mystery shop" the branches to be sure these behaviors are in place. If not, we take those falling short through a review process that helps them build commitment and effective practices. No matter how grand your vision for the future, you have to discover and manifest how that vision translates into day-to-day disciplines and actions. We work on building commitment every day.

When we are hiring, we want to be sure new team members fit. Our family plays polo, and, in fact, is the first to field four generations on a team. Now, I am not comparing people to horses, but there are many lessons that come out of sports. When I buy a new horse, it is not always the best horse money can buy, but the best horse for me. I look for a horse whose natural traits match with my own. After all, we are a team.

The same is true for business partners, employees, or other people who might help you manifest your new future.

Photo courtesy of Larry Senn

LARRY SENN: *Founder and Chairman, Senn Delaney Leadership*

Larry Senn has been my mentor and friend for thirty years. He founded Senn Delaney Management Consulting along with Jim Delaney, who died some years ago. They were number one in the retail reengineering space, but he found that often a CEO client would undo many of the improvements the firm implemented, or stop them in midstream.

So he started Senn Delaney Leadership to work with CEOs and the executive teams to help them align their strategy, structure, and organizational culture. I believe I was the fifth employee in this leadership firm. In the early 1980s we had to define what corporate culture was. Larry transformed me from a manufacturing turnaround guy, often with grease under my fingernails, to a leadership consultant to the CEOs and executive teams of Fortune 500 companies.

Recently, he called me out of the blue to tell me the following, which was exactly what I needed to hear in that moment: "Certain people are consumed by what is in front of them, and others, in moments of stillness, can see beyond to what could be. Paul, you are one of those people."

You will excuse me for saying to Larry in this chapter what I have said to him every quarter since I built my own unique practice: Larry, you made a huge difference in my life, and much of what I have, both spiritually and physically, is due to your support and belief in me.

When I asked Larry to explain how he invented his future, and the future of Senn Delaney, here's what he said:

> *The biggest influence in my life was the way I was raised by my mother. What she said over and over again was that we are born in the image and likeness of God, that our natural state is to be wise and to be loving.*
>
> *We took every employee in Senn Delaney in groups of about ten and had them spend three days on the topic of "purpose" in general, and their own personal purpose specifically. It is just wonderful to see all the different kinds of purposes. I always try to help people I come in contact with to fulfill their vision. People have purposes in all kinds of ways, but usually it is about making a difference for somebody else or for something else. Your purpose can take all kinds of forms.*
>
> *Whether we know it or not, everywhere we go and with everyone we touch, we radiate energy. There is an energy field around us that is contagious. It affects others, and so it becomes incumbent upon us to know that we are the message—that our spirit, our state of mind, our mood, or our energy is the message we are sending.*
>
> *We have a data bank of information in our heads, and we reprocess it over and over again. The question is where do you get original thought? Where did I get the idea to invent an industry called culture shaping that previously did not exist? It did not come from an analytical thought. It came from a different place. When I quiet my mind, somehow I tap into something, and that is where I find a new way to look at things. I learn to see beyond the box, and it is also where I renew myself.*
>
> *When people are at their best, they tend to be more purposeful. They tend to be more about others than themselves. When we are at our worst, when*

we are insecure, we are worried and impatient, and it tends to be all about us. There is a relationship between purposefulness, being at your best, and having a quieter mind.

I was in gymnastics when I attended UCLA. As you may know, gymnastics scores are determined by judges. It was only when I no longer knew the judges were there, when I no longer knew the crowd was there, when I just connected with my art, my performance, that I could truly perform.

For me it was floor exercise. I would be nervous. I would look at the judge, and he would nod his head, and somehow I had to just immerse myself in what I was going to do. When I became conscious of how I was doing, I did not do as well. I think life is like that.

When you came to us you were a diamond in the very rough. You needed a lot of work. But because you were always open to coaching and feedback, I knew that there was nothing I couldn't teach you. And teaching people like you is what contributed to my purpose of building a company that makes a difference in the lives of people and the performance of organizations.

I am at my highest when I am talking about the work I do with people. When I am doing that, I am in a flow state. It is when I am connected to my purpose that I am at my best. I have access to an intelligence beyond myself. It is so startling that at times I say, "where did that come from?"

Photo courtesy of Guy Marsala

GUY MARSALA: *Chief Executive Officer, EZ Lube, and Turnaround Specialist*

Guy Marsala is a professional turnaround expert. He specializes in working with companies that were once great but have lost their way, or that have great potential, but have yet to realize it. These companies need a lot of work to become truly valuable, and the assignments are intense.

He has made a career bringing leadership skills learned as a West

Point–trained Army officer and Fortune 500 executive to middle-market companies. He has had successful assignments in publicly traded, family-owned, and private-equity portfolio companies.

Instead of simply inventing his own future, Guy reinvents the future for failing companies.

The first thing he said to me was, "I'm still learning. I make mistakes. I don't have all the answers." He added later, "But I know how to find the answers."

Here's more of what Guy has to say about enlightened leadership:

> *The people working every day in the stores, in accounts receivable, in purchasing, in manufacturing, they know what's going on, and usually their collective knowledge provides the answers.*

> *People say to me, "How could you go from medical supplies, to soft drinks, to office products, to uniforms, to career education, to quick lubes"? The reason is I listen to customers and the people doing the work. I ask a lot of questions, and discover the problems, the opportunities, and many of the solutions. In the process, I also learn a great deal about the employees, their values, and their commitment.*

It was like old home week for me listening to him talk about what I started my career doing. Strangely enough, we both used a similar method.

> *I ask my teams to take a good hard look in the mirror. We are not changing the metrics to fit our sub-par performance. We are going to raise our performance to the standard that the customer expects. Every day we get the customer satisfaction scores, and every day the whole leadership team reads all of them. The comments also go straight to the stores every day.*

> *What starts happening is, if we do not send the scores to the stores, they call and ask where they are. So if you get your car serviced at an EZ Lube and complete the customer feedback form, the store gets it, as does the*

whole organization. This process empowers the store managers and they quickly take ownership for the performance of their teams.

What I have been able to do is go into a company and figure out pretty quickly what it needs. What's working? What's not working? I call it my deep dive. I talk to everybody, visiting stores, wandering around, chatting with employees, and speaking with customers. It is a very intense thirty to forty-five days of just trying to turn over every stone, finding out what is going on. Once they trust that I'm truly listening and that I'm not going to shoot the messenger, it is amazing what people tell me.

I then report the feedback to the organization: "This is what I heard. Please tell me if I heard you correctly or if I missed anything." After we talk about that, I say, "Okay, if this is where we are today, what are we going to do about it?" That becomes the basis for kicking off the development of OUR (not Guy's) plan. That accelerates the process of people buying-in. Over time the problems and answers become obvious. (It's the consistent execution that is the hard part!)

At EZ Lube it was obvious that, if we were going to succeed, we were going to have to listen to the customer. They told us loud and clear that, above all else, they wanted four things: be fast, be friendly, get it right the first time, and be competitively priced. Once we understood that, excelling on those four customer needs drove all of our initiatives.

We have to work hard, but we are excited to do that in order to make car care easy ("EZ") for our customers. When I combined my knowledge of retail with what I heard from the managers, employees, and customers, it was clear that these four things—fast, friendly, economical, and getting it right the first time—had to become our Non-Negotiable Imperatives. We put it on a large poster, signed it, and we asked all our managers to sign it, store by store, department by department. The poster hangs in the training room and it is the home page on all our computers.

Over time everyone acknowledges how important these things are to our success, because they were part of creating the imperatives. If you cannot follow them, or will not follow them, you cannot work here. Period! I changed half the store managers in a year and a half, and brought in a first-class leadership team, because I know I can't do it alone. It takes a great team and we need everybody pulling hard on the oars in the same direction. I have never been able to get the A+ results with the B– team.

Regarding inner stillness: You know I come from the United States Military Academy. I was an officer in the Army for six years. I had great training in being able to perform under pressure. I might have a cement mixer going on in my stomach, but outwardly, I can appear very calm, disciplined, measured, and consistent. I am not going to fly off the handle, but it would be a big mistake for people to mistake my calmness for complacency. People know when I'm angry. I don't have to shout, they know if they are not living by the core values they said were so important. They are empowered but with that empowerment comes accountability.

JAMES HANKLA: *Retired Head of the Long Beach Harbor Commission, and Long Beach City Manager*

James Hankla literally transformed the City of Long Beach. He led a massive buildup and modernization of the downtown area and the city in general. He is a legend in city government. When he left after a successful run as Long Beach City Manager, he had transformed

Photo courtesy of James Hankla

the harbor, modernized rail access, and started a green program that reduced pollution in the city and beyond.

Here is the story James told me during our interview:

I knew in college, when I was nineteen years old, that I would one day become the city manager of Long Beach. When the offer came, even though being Los Angeles County Supervisor was a great job with lots of perks, I took it. I knew that my personality and skills were perfect for the job, and moreover, it seemed destined.

I knew it when I was a senior in college, when I was working part-time as an intern for the budget research division for the city. I also worked as a recreation area director for Los Angeles County Parks and Recreation. I knew as a budget office intern that the model under which I wanted to serve as an executive was the Long Beach City Charter, because it had a lot of very forceful roles for a city manager.

Although at first I was certain that I was going to succeed the city manager of Long Beach, when I left the area in 1980 to go back to Virginia, I figured, "Well that's it," and I got involved in other things. Still, I stayed in contact with several of the council people and leaders in the community. I was in touch with them all the time.

I never burned bridges. When I came back to the area it was with Campbell Corporation, a Canadian homebuilder that made a lot of money. However, that turned out to be a short period of time because the organization was run terribly, and while I was there, I was recruited by Los Angeles County to be Director for Community Development.

Two and a half years later, I was encouraged by Long Beach's chief administrative officer to apply for this job, and I became City Manager at forty years of age, just as I knew I would be one day when I was nineteen. You have got to be careful what you ask for. People ask me, "How did you know?" The answer: I just had a feeling.

City Manager is about policy and potholes. You've got to attend to both of those things. But if you are a city manager, you can get your team marching in the same direction. You cannot do that at Los Angeles County. It is just too big and too unyielding. For example, at the county we had put up a ballot proposition for four supervisors, but went into the election with only three. We lost that election 49 percent to 51 percent. The unions pulled out all the stops, going back to the "spoil system," because we were taking all the middle managers out of Los Angeles County service.

If we had gotten that, then the county would have been manageable. Around then is when I got the offer to come back to Long Beach. It sounded good to me. With Los Angeles County I was the sixth supervisor. I had a suite of offices with an apartment in the back. I had all of these status symbols. Still, I left anyway. That was my indication that my ego was not as important as my earlier dream.

When I left Long Beach to become the Harbor Commissioner, I didn't feel I had left any unfinished business there. I have a good friend who was a presiding judge at Orange County Superior Court. He was a classmate of mine in college and he said, "You're the only guy I ever knew who said what he was going to be and became it.

LLOYD WALLIS: *President, Rubbercraft*

Lloyd Wallis more than tripled the size and profits of Rubbercraft by developing his team, trusting his intuition, and driving his business with a compelling picture of possibility.

Regarding commitment, he always says, "Ask yourself, on a scale of one to ten, have you done everything possible to achieve your goal? This will tell you how committed you really are."

Photo courtesy of Lloyd Wallis

Here is Lloyd's story about commitment:

> *We came across an opportunity through a combination of past activities, luck, and good timing. We seized the moment. We could have just thought about it, checked it out, and gathered all the traditional information, or said no.*

> *There was going to be a meeting of the decision-makers who were searching for a way to accomplish something groundbreaking on the new Boeing Dreamliner, and the timing was now or never. I knew this would be a great opportunity—one for which we had built a compelling case on two levels. One was working internally with my organization, which I had built upon a dream rather than just another project. That was a little bit like why*

people buy lottery tickets. "Wow, look at what it could be." The second was that I was prepping our corporate parent to see this once-in-a-decade opportunity as a huge return for the risk and capital required. Running numbers in three or four minutes, we could show that we had the opportunity to double, triple, or quadruple the company.

In this case, it was up to me to comprehend, recognize, and launch this opportunity. Because of the short timeframe set by the customer, we had to develop internal support and buy-in without waiting for the typical market studies. Even without much data (that mostly didn't exist), we created an excitement and focus so we didn't miss this very short window of opportunity. In a fast winner-take-all evaluation, Boeing was setting a new direction for the materials and methods of making aircraft that will rule the next several decades. We needed to be the best, and the baseline solution from the beginning.

The development of this opportunity was very much like a "skunk works." Our customers were moving fast, changes were made quickly, and the bureaucracy was limited. And while we had confidence in the long term of the program, we ensured that it was "good business" at every step. If the program direction later changed, it had still been a great moneymaker every step of the way.

It was challenging to sell my "intuitive confidence" in this rare opportunity to those who often held the purse strings but made their decisions analytically. The obvious sometimes required "high-persuasion selling" to ensure "right decisions." While often difficult, no pain no gain. If you truly believe, persevere and fight for it!

In the aerospace industry it is often said, "He who controls the tooling controls the deal." As the program progressed and the customer's capital budgets were stretched, we were pressured to provide tooling at no charge. I saw this as a great opportunity—include the tooling costs with the parts price (we recouped our costs on the first order), own (and control) the tooling, and the baseline selling price going forward is higher! But what I saw as a great opportunity, some saw as cost, risk, and "inconvenient" from a bookkeeping perspective. I was surprised and amazed that anyone would push back on such a strong business case. It's what the customer wanted, a great deal for us, and the bookkeeping was irrelevant from the merits of the cash flow.

With the company's and my own credibility on the line, this issue became a test of commitment. It fell to me to voraciously "sell" it to the owner and board members. Within the framework of what is legal and fair, I had to show that we would do "whatever it takes" to make it happen. When you know something is right you just have to decide, and not quit until you push it through.

Don't ask me now how we moved the thinking from "maybe we shouldn't be in this business" to having profits from the start. We also overcame the initial doubts in investing two or three hundred thousand dollars, knowing it would make another three or four million, even twelve and fifteen million over the program life. It was absolutely essential that I saw the opportunity and committed to it. In turn, this brought the confidence and support of the entire business team. Had I not personally, totally, and visibly committed and accepted accountability, this great opportunity would probably have been lost.

Sometimes big return opportunities that occur in the business world unfold quickly. You have to strike quickly and trust your gut. You have to jump in, commit to it, and work in a sustained manner over time.

We made the choice between an easier but mediocre path that could have meant decline or even failure, or believing and committing to what we knew, and communicating that hope of the future. We had to have faith that we knew we could, and would, deal with the issues and challenges that come up.

Always I ask myself, "Have I really done everything that I can do? On a scale of one to ten, is my commitment a two or a ten, or a thirty?"

Photo courtesy of Heath Clarke

HEATH CLARKE: *Founder, Former Chairman, and Chief Executive Officer at Local Corporation*

Heath Clarke leads Local Corporation, an online advertising company that specializes in local search, a very fast moving industry. He founded the company, in March 1999, and has served as chairman and CEO since January 2001.

Here's how Heath conceived this company:

I read voraciously while I lived in Australia — a chapter each night on my reading chair in the corner of my living room. When I moved to the United States, I went shopping for a new reading chair and ended up in selecting one made of beautiful leather, but it was about AU$4,500 (I was still converting everything back to Australian dollars in those days) — too expensive for me. It occurred to me that I could possibly buy this chair directly from the manufacturers at a lower price, so I obtained a name from the label underneath the pillow, and then went onto the Internet to look up the firm. I couldn't find it, and that sparked the founding idea for this company: There's got to be an easier way for a consumer to connect with a business.

I wrote a business plan in the next 90 days, and founded the company within six months. Our original business model was based on a downloadable toolbar that allowed consumers to search more easily for products and services from their own desktop.

At that point, online advertising was almost entirely national. Ultimately people spend their time and money locally, so we realized that search was "going local." We took it a step further, however, realizing that search was ultimately going to be mobile — i.e. via your phone. We wrote a half-dozen patents in 2002 in what I felt would be a natural advertising model in mobile local — pay per call advertising.

We were fortunate to have a successful IPO in 2004 and saw our stock run from $8 to over $31 within a few months. I finally bought my reading chair *and it's in our offices now for our employees to see why the company was founded!*

In October 2008, we saw a material and sustained shift in the spending patterns of our advertising customers. We had to adapt quickly. We laid off people — never an easy thing to do — and focused on rapidly retooling the business. As we now know, in the fourth quarter of 2008, the great recession began ... but we were ready. We started hiring again in December, and had a record 2009 and 2010. A competitor three times our size who wasn't able to make the shift went out of business.

In 2013 we generated about $100 million in revenues, but our market is changing again, rapidly. Within four years, 80 percent of local searches will be done via a mobile device. Pay-per-call advertising is expected to be a key model in this environment, generating $8 billion in revenues by 2018. We were fortunate to receive five patents in this space in the intervening years so are well positioned to receive royalties in this rapidly growing space, but we have to retool and reinvent our business.

People don't like change, but change is ultimately progress. It's not how big you are — it's how rapidly you can adapt. We've been very lucky to have developed a real-time business with a team that embraces change.

MARK PARRISH: *President, Igloo Products Corporation*

Mark Parrish is an ex-military commander who specializes in building commitment-based cultures. Like a combat-ready unit, he builds teams that are committed to each other's success. It works in mortal combat, and also on business teams.

Photo courtesy of Mark Parrish

Here Mark explains how he builds a strong level of commitment to success:

In his work, The Servant Leader, *James C. Hunter defines discipline as the practice of that which comes unnaturally. Before the beginning of what became the Great Recession, the housing market had already sunk into a deep depression. Against unfavorable economic headwinds, our team chartered a course for a remarkable turnaround in an OEM supplier of residential window and door components. We created this industry-leading turnaround by embracing disciplines which enabled each and every associate the opportunity to transition from simple involvement to complete commitment. As we used to say in the Army, they were afforded the opportunity to "be all that they can be."*

The last thing anyone in troubled times should do is give up the fight for the ideal in favor of accepting their unsatisfactory situation. I call conceding in such fashion "satisficing"— being satisfied with one's current reality at the expense of sacrificing a desired future state. Organizational turnarounds demand collective commitment to a shared future vision. Such visions provide a source of hope, and collective commitment fuels the challenging journey ahead when individual hope may at times be dashed.

Regarding the role of hope on humanity, I've heard it said, "People can survive seven weeks without food, seven days without water, seven minutes without air, but not one second longer without hope." While the numbers may be disputed, the message cannot. Tenaciously leading towards a shared vision by role-modeling commitment to the collective purpose provides hope for others, and is a critical leadership responsibility in creating synergies and delivering team success.

There are three times in which followers expect their leaders to lead: when bestowing rewards and recognition, when painting a vision, and in times of crisis. In those situations, people will remain committed to the difficult journey before them when they see their leader is leading from the front.

Humility is a critical leadership virtue. I recall onboarding at a company in what was, for me, a new industry. While I was comfortable "knowing what I knew," I was acutely aware that I did not know the industry. To lead as though I did would prove, at worst, arrogant, and, at best, inauthentic.

Active listening sessions (to first hear, evaluate, understand, and then reply) proved the seminal step to "Knowing What I Don't Know." In my first three months of employment I made every effort to demonstrate deep respect for the incumbents, personally meeting with sixty-seven people in diverse roles across the organization. We met in one-on-ones, where I listened to their stories and shared the commitment-building disciplines upon which I was so reliant. This intimate experience allowed me to gain unfiltered insights into what was valued most by others in the company. From these meetings I was able to develop a compelling picture of our shared future – a portrait painted by the very words and thoughts of the associates themselves. Through this approach, the path forward became OUR path forward.

Once associates commit to clearly articulated principles, those built upon a shared set of values, the synergies of true teamwork can then be recognized. Even if, early on, some fail to embrace the overall vision, these principles form an expectation, a code of conduct, and define an emerging culture by providing a virtual compass on character that demands candor.

In a TED talk, Derek Sivers said, "The first follower transforms one lonely nut into a leader." He eloquently elaborates on the role of followership, emphasizing that one must first give up the comfort of familiar tribal norms to follow a newly identified leader into an unknown and uncertain future. It takes both personal courage and strength of character to follow another effectively.

One of the first lessons of leadership taught to cadets at West Point is that of excellence through followership. Cultural transformation at its core relies upon faithful followership. A leader must provide a clear vision, defining a path to it for others, in order to give the gift of faithful followership. If colleagues understand their leader is fully committed to the collective success, they're more willing to take a leap into that unknown.

Every written order in the contemporary military is issued following a standard format. While most might relate to the portion known as the mission statement, detailing who is to do what, where, when, and how, it's a lesser-known paragraph called "the commander's intent" that contains the all-important "why." This intent supplants the entire mission statement and serves as the soldier's prime directive. To illustrate, imagine an Army incurs casualties while storming across an airfield en route to high ground, only to later discover the commander's intent of taking the high ground in the first place was to create an airstrip? To lead successfully, organization leaders must constantly ask, answer, and advocate "What is our primary purpose? What is our commander's intent?"

In businesses, strategies and mission statements provide this same clarity by describing the CEO's intent for the enterprise. Effective strategy statements can themselves prove empowering, meaning constrained liberation or "freedom with fences." These messages inform employees what the company is willing to do, and just as importantly, what the company is not willing to do to acquire, retain, or expand its customers. By leveraging strategy statements to their fullest, a sales team, for example, might aggressively seek clients that fit well the strategy and commander's intent, rather than wastefully pursuing the next-best prospect (that does not fit the intent). The question we must always ask is, "Is this client or prospect in line with our strategic intent?" While customers are always right, not everyone is meant to be our customer.

Being personally present in the market enables leadership to observe first hand whether this intent is fulfilled and aligned with ever evolving market trends. As markets evolve, company leaders must demonstrate the courage to let go of ineffective strategies, to maintain that courage with current clients or prospects no longer fitting the aged intent, and to stave off distractions that may lead to satisficing.

Followers must know where their leadership is coming from in order to buy into where the leaders are taking them. I therefore make every effort to articulate to all stakeholders the principles by which I make decisions. Transparency fuels followership.

I believe the goal of business is to build shareholder value by creating a venture which, if it existed today, would put the current market leader out of business, and that the key to doing so is creating a culture worthy of each associate's full commitment.

I further believe that the path to this culture lies in inspiring collective commitment to a shared set of values and rules, or disciplines, defined as the practice of that which comes unnaturally. The results of this approach are both predictable and typically unprecedented.

The art of leadership, therefore, relies upon practicing a handful of virtuous culture-building disciplines while articulating the values-based principles by which decisions shall be made.

MATT WITTE: *Managing Partner, Marwit Investment Management LLC*

I believe that intention works to create the future when you are connected to your purpose, or who you are meant to be.

RICHARD DILDAY: *Chief Executive Officer, Kardent: Design, Planning and Management*

When something goes wrong, I do not sit in my car and shake. What's the point? I get on with it.

Your Calling

After putting all the employees in his company through workshops to find their purpose, Larry Senn marveled at how different each was, yet "all had to do with making a difference for someone or something."

It is important to remember that a calling or purpose is, as Lawrence Koh said, "a resonance," not a specific profession.

Studies indicate that if the ego is not involved, the chances of success are higher. A calling is not a brash grand plan. Jim Hankla stated, "it is a feeling." One of my friends, Gary Mack, better known as "Bat Mack" to professional baseball players, was a sports psychologist who passed away some time ago. He worked in professional baseball and football. His clients were all very successful—you would know their names.

Gary told me he did a study to determine what kind of person would be most likely to succeed in the big leagues. What should a scout be looking for? His study determined that the guys who proclaimed, "I'm gonna be a big star" or "I'm gonna be a hitter or a great fielder—I'm gonna be great" never made it. Their egos got in the way at some point.

He studied, and later worked with, a player that not only made it to the big leagues, the Baltimore Orioles, but never missed a game, and was one of the most consistent hitters and fielders ever. Early on he had realized that baseball was his calling, and what that felt like. Here is what his compelling pictures of his future looked like: Gary said, "They were realistic, and based on his natural gifts."

My friend described it like this: "You know, I think I will be in the big leagues because I am a really good fielder, and a consistent hitter." Gary said, "From the beginning, he had a confidence, and he could see himself in the big leagues. He could see what his skills would naturally bring to the big leagues, and how he could contribute. But he wasn't all wrapped up in his ego about it. He had a calm and authentic intent that drove his practices, career decisions, and games."

Gary taught the scouts to look for those who could articulate their vision in this way. His book is called *Mind Gym*.

The next chapter is designed to help you find and begin the process of becoming your calling. Reflect on what hints life has been whispering in your ears, or shouting, that you might have missed.

PART ONE

KNOW
YOURSELF

Chapter 1

Become Your Calling

How often do you see your calling shining through you, and walk right past it. You hear it like a soft flute lost in the violent concerto of your life, and are swept up by circumstances or someone else's dream. I have vacillated between my father's dream for me and my own calling. Then I realized my calling is not what I did, but how I did it.

John O' Donohue in his book *Beauty* said, "The failure to follow one's calling to creativity severely damages one's spirit." Throughout the rest of the book, I will help you discover your calling. As the book progresses I will help you invent a future that is an expression of your natural genius and calling, no matter what you do for a living.

1: Become Your Calling

"Look inside yourself and your company ... what am I good at and what am I not good at?"

—Stanton J. Rowe, Corporate Vice President, Advanced Technology, and Chief Scientific Officer, Edwards Lifesciences

"A person's gift is just behind their wounds."

—Tony LoRe, Founder, Youth Mentoring Connection

"Every day I discover yet a deeper and more wondrous understanding. There is no limit to what you can experience on the spiritual level. No limit! None!"

—Sydney Banks, spiritual teacher and author

"Before enlightenment you carry water and chop wood. After enlightenment, you carry water and chop wood."

—Zen master

Know Yourself

I was telling my chiropractor, Dr. Wolff, about Bonnie and me walking the annual Belmont Shore car show in Long Beach, California. I had said to Bonnie, "I enjoy these car shows, but they attract so many old people," and she had responded, "They are all our age."

My chiropractor said, "I know what you mean. My staff was telling me I looked just like someone in a magazine they had, and when they showed it to me I was shocked. That person was much older. My staff just gave me a look. So later I took the magazine into the bathroom and held it up beside my reflection in the mirror. I was shocked again. The person in the picture did look like me and we were the same age—I might even have been older. I was seeing myself in the mirror looking like I did fifteen years ago, hair and all."

This happens to many of us. We actually distort reality, like the person at a party who thinks he or she is a great dancer, yet looks clumsy and forced. In dancing it is totally harmless, but these kinds of distortions can be a problem as we continue our journey. If we think we are great at something when we are actually average, we might spend a lifetime trying to succeed at something we will never be able to master. In my experience, this is one of the big reasons why many people struggle to invent their future. They do not really know themselves.

Most successful people have found out what they are naturally good at and have expanded that gift into mastery. They build their career or business around their natural genius, and get help from others who have mastered the abilities that they themselves are not naturally good at. This seems simple, but once our ego decides we are or are not good at something, it fights to be right, even in the face of failure and success. The last thing our ego will say to us is "This is your fault." No, our egos always look for someone or something else to blame, rather than be wrong.

> *"Be the very best that you can be, because you can't lead anybody if you can't lead yourself. You have to be honest with yourself about your good qualities, your bad qualities, and the things you need to work on."*
> —G. J. Hart, CEO, **California Pizza Kitchen**

The ego is designed to protect us. Unfortunately, the only data it has is past experiences. When something occurs that may be similar to a past experience, good or bad, our ego will react in a positive or negative manner. Following the ego's advice may keep us safe, but it is directly in the way of change or risk, which are both essential to inventing a life that differs from the one we are living now.

With these and other defense mechanisms in place, knowing yourself can be easier said than done. This is why even champions who are expanding their natural genius have coaches and mentors. No matter how perceptive she might be, a golfer cannot see her own swing.

It is hard to see ourselves, so being open to feedback is critical to knowing our true nature. While it is important to choose people with wisdom and skill to supply this feedback, in essence everyone can be a mirror. Every reaction is feedback. Every little pain or weakness in an athlete's body is feedback that leads that individual to more balance or practice. How comfortable we feel in our skin in different situations is feedback. Our lack of, or feeling of, wellbeing or pain is feedback.

Feedback is critical to knowing ourselves and where we stand in any endeavor, but it is not enough to invent our futures. We must know who or where we are to begin any journey. We must take the first step into the unknown. But it takes courage to step away from where we are, or who we are. Columbus thought the world was round, but did not know until he left the comfort of the civilized world for the unknown. He sailed a small wooden ship into an ocean that had swallowed many other such craft that had only stayed close to known shores. Are you willing to let go of who you think you are, and find your natural genius?

Discover Your Own Voice

There is a rhythm and flow to every life. When we become an expression of our own natural genius, we dance naturally to the rhythm and flow of the moment. Singers often hit the top of the charts when they stop copying their idols and find their own voice. For example, when Bruce Springsteen began his career, he molded himself after Bob Dylan. He did not become "The Boss" until he found his own voice. This is true in any expression or career. Remember, it is not what you do, but how you do it that is your calling.

> *"We're most imaginative when we're being ourselves."*
> —G. J. Hart, CEO, California Pizza Kitchen

Rosemary Cullinan, a school teacher, took over a failed cafe in my neighborhood and transformed it into a place that guests consider part of the community. You will enjoy this story about someone who was out of work, waitressing and doing odd jobs, and spending her savings. She decided to invest what was left of her savings and buy this failed cafe.

On her restaurant's one-year anniversary, I asked her about what hints her early life may have given her that she missed. After some thought, she told me that when she was three years old she watched her mom make a lemon meringue pie, and learned to make it herself.

At eight she had a regular lemonade stand to make extra money. When she was in college pursuing her father's dream for her, she waited tables to earn money. She would always ask the cooks how they made things, and go home and try out dishes on her friends. Clearly, the signs were there for Rosemary, but she didn't recognize them for what they were at first.

I have known my calling since I was 14 when our priest, the bishop, and the archbishop laid their hands on my head and blessed me during my confirmation. I was surrounded by a deeply peaceful radiance that seemed endless. Even though it only lasted a minute, it seemed much longer, and I did not want to come back. I felt, at the time, that I was meant to share the wisdom that came to me in that moment. As time went on I lost touch with that feeling.

Later in life I met a man named Sydney Banks who was truly an enlightened being. Once he leaned over the table and said to me,

> *"Every day I discover yet a deeper and more wondrous understanding. There is no limit to what you can experience on the spiritual level. No limit, Paul! None!"*

Although I came from humble roots, being committed to deeper learning is my true calling. Each new year I have learned more about how to connect and live from that perspective. A reminder seemed to come out of the blue one afternoon, once I increased my level of commitment to this principle. One of my longtime mentors, Larry Senn, Founder of Senn Delany Leadership, called and casually told me,

"There is something I want to tell you. Certain people are consumed by what is in front of them, and others, in moments of stillness, can see beyond to what could be. Paul, you are one of those people."

I nearly fell off my chair. But as he said it, I knew it to be true. When I work with clients I can see how things will turn out if nothing changes. I can also easily see how certain actions will create a future that fits into their dreams or business goals. It has always been a natural gift. Even in little things. I can fix anything. My wife Bonnie calls me "MacGyver."

Now, as I more fully live my calling, its power shows up in whatever I do for a living. I will be sharing my journey and the journey of others. When I truly connected with my calling, everything, as Goethe suggested, just seemed to happen. Now that calling is deepening and I am listening even more.

Every time I got off the path of my calling, life became more difficult, or I would get a call or email from my dear friend, Norman Wolfe, reminding me about my true course.

Tony LoRe, CEO and founder of the Youth Mentoring Connection, told me:

> *"It takes a monumental amount of effort and labor and work to run this organization. People ask me why I don't burn out, and people warn me that I am gonna burn out. My answer is always I don't believe I can burn out if I am always in my purpose. If I stray from my purpose or calling, I don't get the energy. My vision, my reason for being, my passion gives me all the energy I need."*

Unlike Tony, sometimes I recognized my calling and changed directions, and at other times I just suffered for years. When you are not becoming an expression of your calling, life is difficult. When you are following your calling, life seems like magic is at work. So take time to notice when you are drained by an activity, and when you are inspired. The feelings within you are messages. Your calling is always dropping hints into your conscious mind, even though you might often ignore them.

As already quoted in the Prologue, Lawrence Koh, President of International Diversified Products, said,

> *"So if I sit around and think of ways to make money, that is likely going to be very difficult. But if I am looking for something that inspires me, that resonates to my purpose, that gives meaning to my life and enables me to contribute through serving, then a huge bed of ideas will begin to surface in my awareness, and opportunities related to these ideas will begin to present themselves."*

If you create something that is an expression of your natural gifts, then you will feel great, move with grace and ease, and be prepared to recognize opportunities as they arise. You can work day and night and still be filled with energy. People will see that you love what you are doing and become committed to your mission.

What Hints are You Missing?

If I look back on my life, hints were all over the place. The people I most admired as a young man were writers, poets, and philosophers. I loved playing Robin Hood as a child, and on a number of occasions I would almost merge with nature as I sat in the woods behind our orchard. I did not major in business in college. Instead, I majored in literature and philosophy.

Sometimes it is too late to make a big change, but not often. Look back over your life and think about the things you loved to do. This will point to your calling. But remember, Rosemary's calling, which you will hear more about later, is not running a cafe. It is this:

> *"My calling and joy is being in service to people, and I can do that in many ways. This just fits with my love of food. Dining together is an emotional experience. Breaking bread together in a lovely place with friends is one of life's great pleasures."*

Chef David LaFevre, owner of two top restaurants in Los Angeles, had a similar experience. When he was younger, his guidance counselor in Wisconsin suggested that he get an engineering degree. So, he went to college, but after a short time, he remembered his dream in middle school about being a chef.

> *"I knew in middle school that I wanted to learn how to cook from my mother. I knew I enjoyed doing it. I did not know anything about how to do it. I just knew the result."*

For the longest time I kept my love of poetry and philosophy in the background, thinking it would not work in business. But once I combined my natural love for understanding the true nature of things, which is the purpose of philosophy, with my coaching of leaders, my practice and life blossomed. It began with a commitment to my natural loves.

The first sales call I made after this commitment went well. When the CEO asked what I did, instead of just telling him what I figured he wanted to hear, which was my normal practice, I went into a deeply philosophical explanation. I explained how science has proven that all things are connected by a force that is beyond time and space; that, as a CEO, each of his actions had a ripple effect either creating his future or not. I explained that the only portal to the future is the present moment, and that trends can be seen only through the portal of the present.

He stopped me at that point, at which time my ego was having second thoughts about my response, as if saying to me, "I told you so." However, he said, "I have been looking for someone like you all my life." He did not negotiate the fee, which I found out later he had never done, but just asked when we could start the job.

Tame Your Dragons

Throughout my life I have found that I had to face and tame the dragons blocking my connection with my calling. Tony LoRe, who works to help inner-city teens, says, "A person's gift is just behind their wounds." We are guarded by a primal force that often uncontrollably leaps out, like a powerful dragon, to attack anything that might reopen a wound. When our wounds are healed we tame the dragon and this powerful beast naturally protects our gifts, or calling, instead of our wounds.

In the time of the Roman Empire, at birth each person was given a "genius," which was a god who watched over you, a god with whom you could collaborate while traveling in this world. When your heart beats as one with your genius, your travels are filled with creativity and joy. Good fortune seems to radiate from you always. When you listen and respond to your natural genius or calling, a resonance begins.

Lawrence Koh, President of International Diversified Products, says:

> *"Consider the relationship between tuning forks in different notes. If you hit a tuning fork tuned to a C note, and place another tuning fork tuned to the same key next to it, it will begin to resonate or vibrate, even if they're tuned to different octaves. However, if you place next to it a tuning fork tuned to any other note, they will not resonate. Physics has proven that everything in life carries with it a specific particular. In other words, everything has a specific vibratory aspect and, like the tuning forks, this is how 'like attracts like' in life.*
>
> *"This resonance with my purpose or calling rings out authentically in my life and engulfs everyone around me. When I am living my purpose it enables me to be patient and humble with clients and members of my team. The resonance that my purpose or calling carries does much of the work when I allow it to do so."*

The Heartbeat of Life

The first organ that develops in the womb is the heart. With all our science we still do not understand exactly what animates its beat. But we do know there is a mysterious force that animates life itself. If you sit quietly in nature you can feel that force. Call it what you will, but it is the life force that animates your heart, which in turn animates your body by flowing oxygenated blood through your arteries.

When we are unhappy it seems to me that we are out of rhythm with the flow and beat of life itself. While this force continues to animate us, as we put attention on our thoughts about what has happened and what might happen, our energy and radiance falters. Placing our consciousness on these thoughts for too long begins to disconnect us from the life force, and often leads to high levels of stress, causing heart attacks, sudden unnatural death, and illness. We stop dancing to the rhythm of life, which is always there, and our entire system starts to fall apart as we unplug from our power source. It is a natural warning to get back to our unique dance of life.

So when you are feeling stressed, remember the life force that is always present, bringing you and everything around you to life. It is creating a beautiful and diverse creation. Do whatever helps you let go of the thinking that is creating your stress. I cycle to meditation music and ride like the wind. I use my heart to tune myself with the rhythm and flow of life itself. If you let your heart become a tuning fork for the heartbeat of life, and be like a runner whose breathing and heartbeat synchronizes with the body, you will feel a surge of natural energy.

Work on Your Consciousness

Be careful not to let your fear darken your consciousness and paralyze you with depression. Also remember that "pretending not to know" in times of change is deadly. In times of economic change, we all need to be alert and highly conscious to make the right decisions. Having a depressed or irrationally elevated state of mind will only narrow your consciousness, and reduce your chances of inventing a meaningful future for you and your family.

I have carefully prepared this book's roadmap from my personal experience, and the experience of many successful people.

Enjoy the Journey

Our images of the Great Depression are informed by the dispiriting monochromatic newsreels and photographs that were shot at that time. Nevertheless, everything was in color then, of course; we just did not have the technology to capture it. Birds sang in the morning, flowers bloomed in the spring, and each morning the sun would rise with magnificent colors. The flow of "The Great Intelligence" and "the peace that passes all understanding" was, and is, still waiting for us. Even in the Great Depression, people loved each other, kissed in the dark, danced, and laughed. I have been told that communities pulled together in wonderful ways that we don't often experience today.

The moral? Enjoy the journey, no matter where you start from. Trips seem longer when you "can't wait to get there." Presence guided by intention frees us.

This is the essence of the journey we can take in life. We can find the rhythm in the madness. We can walk together into the mystery, and dance with the heartbeat of life, which will reveal your calling.

PRACTICES and ACTIONS

Mike DuRee is the fire chief of the City of Long Beach California, which has close to 500,000 residents. He told me the following story from his childhood.

> *"My great grandfather, who was a Fire Chief, would take me into Station 4 occasionally. I still love the smell of a fire station every time I walk into one. When I was three the station threw me a birthday party, and gave me a little red peddle car which was a miniature fire engine. I loved that fire engine. I took it home and waxed it for hours and kept it clean. My friends had bikes, but until I got too big to fit in it, I always drove this around."*

As you chart your early childhood experiences look for events like this. Clearly, Chief DuRee is living his calling. To know yourself at a deeper level, I suggest charting your life's highs and lows starting with your earliest childhood memories in chronological order. This will provide many insights.

1. For each low, understand how your ego has placed a marker in your psyche to protect you from similar experiences in the present or future. This is valuable because our ego's function is to protect us. For example, if as a child you put your hand into a flame and burned yourself, your ego will send out fear warning signals, which is right and appropriate. Firefighters have to overcome their ego's warnings to charge into a burning building, even when they are wearing protective gear. Our egos make a marker, but do not understand context. The only data point our egos have is a past painful experience. Likewise, a

painful childhood or adult experience will be protected by the ego. But often, like the firefighters, these warning signals of fear simply prevent us from being our best. They often mute our natural genius or gifts. As you chart the lows in your life, look for warning signals in your head that are no longer useful, those that block you from inventing your future. I was bullied in elementary school because I had an English accent and did not know the rules of baseball. Had I not overcome these fears I would not have been able to lead teams of people past their own fears and blocks as I do today.

2. As you chart your highs, look for the very highest states of mind (being "in the zone"), as well those that are simply pleasant. In my experience, these highs will be more difficult to attain, because the ego protects you from fear-based past experiences. So you will have to work harder at remembering your highs. You might ask childhood friends or your parents to remind you of these. My wife Bonnie kept a journal about her son from years one to four. Many of these loving experiences had been forgotten, but came to mind as she read through the journal.

3. Look for the natural entry points to your highest states of your mind. For example one client explained that when he cycled he often entered the zone as he surged to pass people. He said to himself, "let's do it." That triggered his ability to exceed his own expectations. He learned to use that phrase in other circumstances as a trigger.

Notice what inspires you and what you have always been good at. What activities and people draw you into a higher state of mind? As you proceed further through this book, your goal will be to learn how to expand your consciousness around your natural strength and genius. As you recall and understand each of these experiences it will help you understand your natural calling and what holds you back.

Chapter 2:

Discover Your Gifts and Passion

Your calling reveals your natural gifts or genius. Each of us does this in our own way —some, unfortunately, by driving to success while losing life, and others by suppressing their genius out of fear. Protecting that precious gift can mean hiding your light. The "bushel baskets" we hide under come in many colors, but your light is always peeking out, and you can see it if you are looking.

"Your time is limited. Don't waste it living someone else's life."

—Steve Jobs, CEO and Founder, Apple

"Look inside yourself and your company … what am I good at and what am I not good at?"

—Stanton J. Rowe, Corporate Vice President, Advanced Technology, and Chief Scientific Officer, Edwards Lifesciences

"If you are operating from your natural self as a business, and as a leader of that business, I believe that you will attract a tremendous amount of trust and prosperity. You will excel in your field because people will want to be with you, and possibly be more like you, because you are exuding energy that's very positive."

—Casey Sheahan, CEO, Patagonia

"We cultivate our employees instead of trying to change them."

—Lawrence Koh, President, International Diversified Products

Tony LoRe, CEO and founder of Youth Mentoring Connection, once explained to me how his process seeks out a teenager's natural gifts, or as I said in my first book, their "genius." He said that in his work he has found that a person's strongest gift hides right behind his or her psychological wounds. Most often, some childhood event caused that person to hide that gift using the trauma of the wound as a shield. He told this story to illustrate how children naturally know their gift and cannot help but express it, if it is not repressed.

> "Some believe that a person's gift first shows up when you are eight or nine years old, and how the family or community responds to it will determine whether you are going to protect yourself by hiding it away, or expand and live into it.

> "Here is a famous story about Showtime at the Apollo on amateur night. The announcer up on stage said, 'Our next performer is an eight-year-old young lady who is going to dance for us.' Then this little kid comes running across the stage, and whispers in the announcer's ears. 'Oh … correction, she's decided that she's gonna sing, so everybody welcome Miss Ella Fitzgerald.' Her gift was displayed in front of the crowd. She stood in amazement as the applause rang out. Her gift was recognized and she got to live fully into it."

For those of you who may not be familiar with jazz singers, Ella Fitzgerald was one of the greatest singers of all time.

If you are trying to discover your natural gift or genius, it would be wise to go back to your childhood and notice what you loved to do that you documented in the practices and actions section of Chapter 1. Because no matter how deeply you have hidden that gift, it is still there behind all the reasons you buried it. You will not succeed trying to do something that is not your natural gift or genius.

Here is a quote I used in *Unleashing Genius* that summarizes why it is so hard to know your calling.

> *"Our deepest fear is not that we are inadequate. Our deepest fear is that we are powerful beyond measure. It is our light, not our darkness, that most frightens us. We ask ourselves, who am I to be brilliant, to be gorgeous, talented, and fabulous. Actually, who are you not to be? You are a child of God. Your playing small doesn't serve the world. There is nothing enlightened about shrinking so that others won't feel insecure around you. We are born to make manifest the glory of God within us. It is not just in some of us, it is in everyone. And as we let our light shine, we consciously give others permission to do the same. As we are liberated from our own fear, our presence automatically liberates others."*

—**Marianne Williamson,** *A Return to Love*

Know Thyself

Stanton Rowe, Chief Scientific Officer of Edwards Lifesciences, who led the development of a heart valve replacement process that eliminates the need for open-heart surgery, said, "Look inside yourself and your company … what am I good at and what am I not good at?" Knowing yourself is so important to success, yet it's something we often put off until late in life. Those who have successfully invented their futures see it as the first priority.

Tom Davin, CEO of 511 Tactical, is a living example of aligning his work with his natural gifts and passion. A graduate from the Marine Officer Basic School, U.S. Army Ranger School, and the Special Forces Combat Diver Course, with an AB degree from Duke University and an MBA from Harvard Business School, he has used his leadership skills for his board positions and has been CEO of Panda Restaurant Group, Inc.

Tom's office has a gym and showers, and Tom brings in some of the country's top physical trainers to teach at lunch. While he was giving me a tour of the facility, he climbed up about sixty feet on a rope. He clearly could not have been happier about how his business was succeeding. In his words, "We are crushing it." He can't help but synchronize with his market. He and the members of his team are the market for most of his products. Here is part of Tom's philosophy:

> *"Accountability is key here. We seek to achieve results with a bias for action. We like to compete and be measured against the most demanding standards to ensure our continued success."*

Values like this are important compelling pictures to set the tone and motivate an organization. But it is important to remember we all start the journey from a different place. We are all unique individuals, made up of complex forces from the past and the present. No one is exactly the same. We can all become more accountable, but a leader must recognize, that there are as many different ways to get to accountability as there are people.

The biggest mistake most people make is to try to become someone else. Someone can become more accountable, as this compelling picture describes, but not exactly like their leader. Not truly knowing your own starting point and natural genius can make any journey more difficult, and most often impossible. It would be like a five-foot, five-inch tall person wanting to be a star center in the NBA. No matter how much he practiced, or how hard he trained, he would never succeed. Such a person, despite lofty dreams, would be trying too hard and hardly ever succeeding. People who know their natural genius are able to place themselves in positions that demand the things they are really good at. Additionally, and probably most important, they seem authentic and thereby attractive.

If you are operating from your natural self as a business, and as a leader of that business, I believe that you will attract a tremendous amount of trust and prosperity. You will excel in your field because people will want to be with you, and possibly be more like you, because you are exuding energy that's very positive.

The mistake most of us make is not knowing our own gifts or genius. It just makes any mission harder. Who you are is always the starting point to any future you want to create. If you do not know yourself, you start at the wrong point. You are misaligned with reality. When you don't know where you are, a roadmap is useless. All life lessons need to be applied in the context of understanding who you are. Without this knowledge, you may proceed based on an assumption about your skills that may not conform to a grounded reality.

Steve Jobs is often quoted as saying, "Your time is limited. Don't waste it living someone else's life." As I read his autobiography, it became clear that he loved both beauty and engineering. He combined the arts and humanities with business. That was an expression of who he was, and the world rushed to his beautifully designed products and stores.

Before leaders can accomplish anything, they must first understand themselves and present reality, challenge their own thinking, communicate a well-thought-out and concise strategic direction, and define a clear and actionable plan for execution.

The same is true for building a tree house or a career. In my earlier book, *Unleashing Genius: Leading Yourself, Teams and Corporations*, I talked about how to unleash your natural genius. When that process is well underway, then you can begin to invent your future.

Guy Marsala, CEO of EZ Lube and a turnaround specialist said, "I'm still learning. I make mistakes. I don't have all the answers." He added later, "But I know how to find the answers."

All successful leaders will tell you that they are continuously learning about themselves. You are the starting point for every decision you make. If you don't really understand your strengths and weaknesses, that starting point could be wrong. When you start with an unrealistic fantasy about yourself, it is almost impossible to succeed. More important, when you put your blood, sweat, and tears into something that is not who you are, you might struggle and end up somewhere that you hate. I know several people who feel trapped by the choices they've made, but feel it is too late to make any changes.

No matter how much research is done, a leader must make the final call in an organization or individual life. To make that call with confidence, you must know the answer to who you are. Who you are is a manifestation of your calling, as opposed to some identity you may have adopted from your parents and social norms in general. Knowledge of your own strengths and weaknesses will lead you to act from your strengths and enlist others with strengths in the areas of your weaknesses.

Once you know the answer, then you must communicate to those you want to enlist in your journey clearly, simply, and concretely—and in a compelling manner. Only then will people have the faith to follow you.

PRACTICES and ACTIONS

The following practices act as a roadmap for surpassing common business or personal hurdles to achieve success and invent a well-designed future for your business or your life. These steps work for everything from building a porch on the front of your house to improving your happiness, creating a great company, or galvanizing a nation.

> *"Whether we know it or not, everywhere we go and with everyone we touch, we all radiate energy. The energy field around us is contagious. It affects others and so it becomes incumbent upon us to know that we are the message. That our spirit, our state of mind, our mood or energy is the message we are sending."* —**Larry Senn, founder and chairman of Senn Delaney Leadership**

Here are some issues to look into:

1. Examine each painful experience you've had. Then see, as Tony LoRe has suggested, what part of your deepest desires or genius you might be suppressing or "protecting from harm."

2. Examine activities that seem easy and natural to you. We often take these skills for granted, and turn our attention to those activities that seem hard. For example, because I was the oldest son of four children, I learned how to facilitate games with my brothers, and keep them out of trouble when Mom and Dad were away, which was often. But in high school I decided to major in physics, which was far from my natural skills of facilitation and coaching. Luckily, and due to a lot of feedback, I discovered these skills and have made a career out of them.

3. What childhood heroes inspired you? In childhood games I was always Robin Hood helping the oppressed. Now I help teams of people become committed to each other's success.

4. Call your friends and ask them what they see in you that you seem really good at. Write each friend's comments down and look for a pattern; I assure you that you will find one or two.

5. Examine what activities bring you "into the zone"—those things that others might see as work but that you love to do. For example, I love to garden, build things, and to see things grow. It's no accident that I help people grow and invent their futures.

6. What is the nature of your childhood dreams? What dreams did you set aside to become an adult and support your family? While I am not suggesting you change your career, I do suggest that you can apply essences of your dream to whatever you are currently doing.

PART TWO:

DISCOVER
THE ANSWER

Photo: Sarah Clarehart

Chapter 3:

Master the Present

Because the future emerges from the present, you must understand present reality in depth. Each disturbance and opening of the life force ultimately ripples out into the days, months and years ahead. The only way to invent your future is through your mastery of the present ... the good, the bad, and the ugly.

"Knowing others is intelligence; knowing yourself is true wisdom. Mastering others is strength: Mastering yourself is true power. If you realize that you have enough, you are truly rich."

—Lao Tzu, *Tao Te Ching*

"There was something inside me because I had just come from an organization that worked. It flew so high and so fast, and it was a wonderful experience with Giorgio Beverly Hills. It just grew and, wow, I loved it. It was so exciting. I thought I had to bring just a portion of that excitement and enthusiasm, combined in a cohesiveness that is in Giorgio Beverly Hills. I said to myself, 'I'll try to capture that capability in this new organization to help people. And if I can do that, it will really be an exciting thing."

—Linda LoRe, CEO, Frederick's of Hollywood

Photo: Sarah Clarehart

Have you ever seen a new product and said, "I thought of that," or heard that someone was untrue to his or her spouse and knew something would go wrong before it actually did. We live in a small town where retail stores open and close all the time. It is often obvious to us that they will not succeed. We often know the answer to a problem before we admit we do. When you look back on your life I am sure you can find times when you knew something deep down, but somehow your fear or doubt interfered with recognizing that truth consciously.

Years ago my partners and I hired a branding and marketing person who was perfect for what we needed as a firm. The fit was exact. That year we had the annual 5K run at the company meeting. This new person came in way ahead of the CEO and president, both of whom had run marathons earlier in the year. He smoked and had a beer belly, so the results didn't add up in my mind. When I asked him about the race results, he said, "I must have just gotten lucky."

The minute we returned from the trip, I asked the HR person if she had checked his references. The answer was no. I had her check and it turned out that nothing on his resume was true. It was all made up, and on some level I knew. During our debrief we all realized that we had a bad feeling about this guy, but we needed someone in the position so badly, and he seemed like a fit. So, we ignored our knowing. Imagine how much money and time we would have saved if we had acted on our knowing.

As you read in the Prologue, Jim Hankla was a legendary city manager of Long Beach, California and head of the Harbor Commission. Before that he was a Los Angeles County supervisor. He told me in our interview that he knew in college that he would one day become the city manager of Long Beach. When the offer came, even though being Los Angeles

County supervisor was a great job with lots of perks, he took it. He knew that his personality and skills where perfect for the job, and moreover, it seemed destined. He recognized his "knowing" and transformed the city.

Knowledge is to wisdom as a roadmap is to a territory. Knowledge is made up of information and data. It describes, like a roadmap, what has been remembered and written down. But like the roadmap, it is only an approximation of the reality it is describing. We can study all the information, but in the end, we have to use our intuitive mind to make a decision.

Intuition synthesizes both the obvious and hidden drivers. We all have this instinctive ability, but many have lost touch with it. Birds migrate thousands of miles to the same nest each year, dogs know when you are afraid, and salmon find their way from the ocean to the river that leads to the place of their birth. They don't need maps or GPS. Why?

> *"The intuitive mind is a sacred gift and the rational mind is a faithful servant. We have created a society that honors the servant and has forgotten the gift."* —**Attributed to Albert Einstein**

True intuition comes from knowledge, but extends beyond it. It is knowing how to navigate knowledge, and seeing the patterns that lead to a better future. Because we become attached to what we know, or think we know, we often miss the obvious. Jim Hankla knew himself and acted on his intuition which in part is driven by a high level of pattern recognition, and is now an honored elder in his community.

Past Experience Is Not Enough

Many have said that experience is the greatest teacher—but this is not always the case. In times of profound change, when you most need to invent your future, many people rely only on their memories of past experiences to mitigate mounting risk. When the nature and complexity of problems are unprecedented, solutions from past experience are not enough, and may mislead us.

Peter J. Dekom, author and visionary business leader, once said in a lecture that, "Any [financial] research done that is based on data before September 15, 2008 is meaningless."

The financial crisis of 2008 changed everything. Instincts developed prior to major shifts have to retrained. In turbulent times, fear tends to narrow our consciousness and block us from seeing present reality as it unfolds into the future. When our lives are not working out the way we want, we often lose touch with our knowing. Some of my friends call this problem "pretending not to know."

Life is often like shooting rapids. There is a correct course in the currents of change; there are also people who will run you into rocks, and those who will drown you, your life, and your company. Self-knowledge and knowing when you know are essential. We all need to learn to be "in the zone."

Most often our knowing represents a dream bigger than our expectations. It shows us possibilities that seem too good to be true. But many of the leaders I have worked with always say, "A good leader will inspire you to exceed your expectations." Our own expectations of ourselves are often a barrier. If we don't live up to what we know we can do, we will never be happy. By letting our fears dull our knowing, we are ill-prepared when opportunities arise.

> *"Dream big. What's the world of possibilities for yourself and for your organization? You have to be able to say, 'Here's where I want to go.' It's not that you'll ever necessarily get there, but if you don't dream, you'll never even get started.* —G. J. Hart, Chairman and CEO, California Pizza Kitchen

People who succeed in today's volatile world must conquer obstacles the way a championship basketball team does in a "fast break." They overcome insecurities that hold them back, and respond instantly to the flow of the game—knowing when to cut to the basket, or when to pass.

Set your life up for the championship you know you can win, but be sure it is way beyond your present expectations of yourself.

Wisdom, to me, is intuition combined with pattern recognition. When you know, you act naturally in response to the highest good. It is like a person "in the zone," playing for a championship they knew they were meant to experience. Here is the more formal definition:

> **Wisdom n.** *The ability to discern or judge what is true, right, or lasting; insight; common sense; good judgment is a characteristic of wisdom.*

I attended a Bat Mitzvah for my friend's daughter. At the end of the ceremony the Rabbi said to the young girl, "May you become the person God meant you to be." All knowledge starts with discovering your unique genius, or God-given gifts. It is your starting place in life, though you may often forget who you were meant to be. Larry Senn, founder and chairman of Senn Delaney Leadership and one of my mentors said,

> *"We have a data bank of information in our heads and we reprocess it over and over again. The question is where do you get original thought? Where did I get the idea to invent an industry called culture shaping that previously did not exist. It did not come from an analytical thought. It came from a different place. When I quiet my mind, somehow I tap into something, and that is where I find a new way to look at things. I learn to see beyond the box, and it is also where I renew myself."*

Every person I have known who is a living example of their purpose or calling says these kinds of things. They quiet their minds and resonate with who they are, and the answers come flowing into their consciousness.

PRACTICES and ACTIONS

To know yourself at a deeper level, I suggest charting your life's highs and lows starting with your earliest childhood memories in chronological order. This will provide many insights.

1. Go back to your childhood, somewhere between age six and eight, and remember your fantasies and dreams. Write them down in your journal in as much detail as you can remember.

2. In Chapter 2, I suggested that you ask people to tell you what you do well. Now ask these same people what they see you doing that sabotages those strengths. Ask them to suggest things you could improve upon. Write all of this down in your journal without editorial comment.

3. After you have talked with everyone who knows you well, review your notes to understand exactly who you are at your essence. Compare this insight with your childhood dreams. It will provide you with knowledge about yourself and how you act in the world. With that understanding, this book will help you begin expanding your strengths, and stop acting out your weaknesses.

4. Take an hour or so now in a quiet place and look back on all the times you knew that something was wrong or right, but did not act. As you do this, notice the pattern of your thought. Observe what typically stopped you. What is that little voice in your head? Get in touch with the feeling of fear and hesitation, and do the same with times when you acted on your knowing. What was that feeling—the way you felt in your gut?

5. Practice moving from fear to knowing and to acting. First, experience knowing in your imagination, and then practice acting on your knowing in your life. Start with small things and build from there. With practice, you will develop the courage to move out of your fears and act on your knowing. This practice, once mastered, will be key to inventing your future.

There is no substitute for practice when it comes to breaking habitual behaviors. Society has turned us away from our natural instincts and knowing. Remember what Albert Einstein is thought to have said about the intuitive mind being a sacred gift.

Those who have and will build our future will rediscover this forgotten gift and practice until they achieve mastery.

I encourage you to share your stories and insights on the *Invent Your Future* page on Facebook. This will facilitate dialog, build our community, and give you an opportunity to schedule a Skype call with me, or use online tools to help you advance yourself.

Chapter 4

Embrace Wisdom

Wisdom is when knowledge of your natural gifts is expressed in your life, as opposed to just having knowledge of who you are. This knowledge of self is a very important first step, but only the beginning of inventing your future. If you start a journey but do not know where you are, even the best plans will not take you to your destination. The first step in any life is to discover and express your natural genius.

"When something resonates to our purpose in life, when something resonates to a contribution that we want to make, when something resonates to a service that we want to perform, there is a solidity and a recognition that takes place within you. When you follow this resonance, this inner guidance, this experience, it becomes easier to recognize over time. When this resonance is present, it does not matter whether it involves a product, a technology, or a service. The emergence of your purpose, your inner calling will begin coloring your life with a mystical quality and a depth of meaning that far exceeds the goal of making a profit."

—Lawrence Koh, President, International Diversified Products

"When people are at their best, they tend to be more purposeful. They tend to be more about others than themselves. When we are at our worst, when we are insecure, we are worried and impatient, and it tends to be all about us. There is a relationship between purposefulness, being at your best, and having a quieter mind."

—Larry Senn, Founder and Chairman, Senn Delaney Leadership

Photo: Sarah Clarehart

When you look at great singers like Paul Simon, Bob Dylan, James Taylor, Lady Gaga, Diana Krall, Frank Sinatra, Brad Paisley, and others, you find that they are singing the songs with their own voice, which is always unique. Many people start by copying other singers who are close to who they are, but true greatness does not come until they express their own voice. They are expressing their music through who they are, and because we are all unique beings, it is always beautiful. Alignment between your self-knowledge and the way you express yourself is true wisdom. So if you do not know what your natural gifts are, that will be your first quest as you work through this book. Once you know yourself, everything else follows with more ease and grace than you can imagine.

> *"These are things that when they appear we usually say, 'Wow, this is a great idea' (versus a good idea), meaning that though it emerged from within us, it was given to us. When we recognize the spiritual quality of this action, we become profoundly impacted by it. So if I sit around and think of ways to make money, that is likely going to be very difficult. But if I am looking for something that inspires me, that resonates to my purpose, that gives meaning to my life and enables me to contribute through serving, then a huge bed of ideas will begin to surface in my awareness and opportunities related to these ideas will begin to present themselves."*
>
> **—Lawrence Koh, President, International Diversified Products**

Imagine a world, company, or life committed to nourishing every glimmer of this type of wisdom from the cradle to the grave. How would it feel to live in a world whose first priority was seeking and manifesting wisdom? Can you see how wisdom would flourish into genius with waves of innovations that naturally lead to abundance and wealth beyond our imagination today?

Your first challenge will be to find your natural voice or expression. One of my favorite book titles is, *Actualizations: You Don't Have to Rehearse to Be Yourself*, by Stewart Emery. While you have to practice to refine your natural gifts to take them to greatness, your progress will be much faster than trying to copy someone else's style in any endeavor.

Wisdom Is the Seed

I have seen leaders whose teams, once sparked by their wisdom, are like a basketball team "in the zone" on a fast break, committed to a new innovation. I have found a number of important elements on these teams. But the first is wisdom that reveals insight, creates actions, and unleashes wealth and wellbeing. Wisdom is the seed for our field of dreams.

Without discernment of what is true, right, or lasting, most of the innovations that make our world so comfortable and safe would not exist today. For example, the use of fire, the wheel, refrigeration, our communication satellites, the Internet, and planes that can fly from one continent to another.

When great sailing ships, which were technological innovations, were the only way to cross oceans, entire crews were often lost. The dangers to travelers and businessmen were enormous. There was no telling when a ship would be crushed by a storm, or blown into uncharted seas beyond the reach of civilization. Yet some of these ships and the wisdom of the leaders who launched their missions found new worlds and enormous wealth. The commitment took a knowing that was beyond knowledge.

Our collective wisdom has discovered new technologies that have dramatically improved our lives. Now when sailors are lost, we can often find them with a simple global positioning device or even a cell phone.

Wisdom Creates Wealth and Wellbeing

I have worked with CEOs and their teams for more than thirty years. Their biggest challenge is to build teams that create new innovative realities before others have even thought of them. Two minutes of true insight and wisdom can discover realities that can change society, your life, or your company, small or large. A flash of insight into the true nature of something important to the future can create a whole new world, as with Columbus and others who realized that the earth is round.

Once Discovered, Wisdom Looks Obvious

It's true: Once discovered, wisdom seems obvious and when explained to people, they often totally get it. Casey Sheahan, former CEO of Patagonia, after explaining a decision he made about publishing the carbon footprint for all their products on their website, said the following:

> *"When I look back on that decision, the fact that it was smart looks more like 'that guy was just a master of the obvious,' and it seems simple when you actually see what the outcome and the strategy is now. It's like 'wow, that was dumb'... it was right here under our noses."*

The test of a wise decision once discovered is that the insight seems obvious, even though prior to the decision it was almost impossible to see.

Ancient Wisdom

Stone circles created 5,000 years ago are examples of ancient technology. They enabled their creators to predict the seasons and increase agricultural productivity. Someone noticed the position of the sun each season, had an insight, and began laying out stones. Then the technology spread by word of mouth, and the world changed forever. There are remains of more than a thousand wood and stone circles in the United Kingdom today.

Is Seeking Wisdom a Priority for You?

How many of us make the deepening of wisdom a personal, organizational, or national priority? Few, I would say. Have you made seeking wisdom one of the most important commitments in your life? Are you refining your ability to discern or judge what is true, right, or lasting?

Wisdom manifested in action often creates wealth and wellbeing. Yet, we seem to long for wealth and wellbeing without seeking that wisdom first. The desire for wealth and wellbeing is not enough, and mere desire often interferes with wisdom. When wisdom is the priority for an individual or a team that is passionate about a purpose, they create what seem like miracles.

Organizing Wisdom Worldwide

My dream has always been to lead a team of champions in their fields, partnering with leaders, to create wisdom, wealth, and wellbeing on a global scale. To me it is our only choice. How many times has a dream glimmered in your consciousness only to be lost? Have you ever seen a new innovation in your mind's eye but let it go, yet later seeing it implemented by someone else? Companies, societies, and people who do not make wisdom a priority lose great amounts of wealth and wellbeing every day. On the other hand, imagine each person on your team, or in your company, life, and country committed to seeking the wisdom that unleashes his or her own genius and the genius of others. Imagine technologies that could be manifest, and then picture how the world would improve.

The first step is to make creating wisdom, wealth, and wellbeing a priority for yourself. How much easier would it be for children to learn if their teachers were helping them find their natural genius and wisdom? We can all deepen our wisdom and express our genius more often if we start with ourselves and reach success, even after stumbling and falling many times. Even after many post-graduate courses at "Brick Wall University," when we successfully navigate our own waters, we can then help others. As you work on mastering each of these skills, start to envision the compelling future you want to live.

A New Renaissance Could Happen Today

The Renaissance came out of the Dark Ages to create the wealth and wellbeing we have today. Make it a priority in your life to assemble teams of seasoned advisors who have found their natural genius and have wisdom working in their favor. Teams that partner with leaders and investors, who make seeking and manifesting wisdom their first priority, will change our lives. If you do this, you may even seed a new Renaissance in your personal world.

I recommend that you stop wasting time doing anything that does not lead to developing your own wisdom. Make seeking and manifesting wisdom your first priority, and find others who are committed to doing the same. It will be the most fun and exciting thing you have ever done, and we will all benefit from the wisdom you discover.

Ancient Wisdom and New Science

Great poets and philosophers, such as Goethe, have tried for thousands of years to draw our attention to moments from our lives. They try to open our windows of perception. Remember what one of our greatest thinkers said:

> *"I do not invent. I discover realities that were previously undiscovered."*
> —**Albert Einstein**

If certain realities were undiscovered, how did Einstein find them? What realities are yet to be discovered? There have been stories in both ancient and modern literature of wizards, saints, and shamans who affect events from a distance. As a poet, I feel much of my writing comes through me. In fact, I feel I have been compelled, or "called," to write this book. Who is to say what is yet to be discovered?

With the proof of Bell's Theorem, science has discovered informational channels underlying our existence that we refer to as intuition, common sense, and insight. It seems that science has now discovered channels that previously were inconceivable, and that connect everything. We know these channels exist, but we still do not know how to use them.

Something Outside of Time and Space

Quantum physicist Antoine Suarez was quoted in an article in *Discover* magazine regarding a concept he calls entanglement. "In entanglement, two particles become twinned in such a way that the measurement of one always determines the properties of the other, no matter how far apart they may be." Later in the article he says, "You could say the experiment shows that space-time does not contain all the intelligent entities acting in the world because something outside of time is coordinating the photons' results."

In this and a number of other experiments, physics has suggested that all things seem to be connected, and that there are channels of invisible communication that occur instantly. Atoms communicate to each other outside of time and space. Atoms are the building blocks of everything in our world. Like the atoms that communicate without language, so do we. Who is to say when or where our energies begin and end, or from where communication might come? Clearly, forces are at work that we have yet to understand scientifically. Yet do we actually use these forces without knowing?

When you master how to synchronize these discoveries using the present pace of change as an accelerator or sling shot, you enter "the power curve" on the waves of change that are creating new opportunities for some people, and disasters for those who are unaware of their effect. Although more complex, it is much like the sweet spot on a wave where a surfer finds the most acceleration.

What if we could project our intentions into this timeless force and affect the molecular structure of our bodies? That would explain the well-documented healing of cancer patients and others outside of the parameters of traditional medicine. What if we could transfer our energies into the heart of others, the way men and women do when they fall in love? Many people feel that prayer works. Does prayer travel through this quantum force? What if leaders could attract customers to buy their products using this force? What if we could travel using this energy? We could literally find ourselves anywhere in the world or universe instantly. This is a bit far out, but who knows what remains undiscovered?

Having worked with successful CEOs most of my adult life, I have seen many things become reality that most people would think impossible. You, too, can discover new realities with practice.

Find a Wise Teacher

Leaders, kings, and emperors have had wise teachers whispering the hidden truths of the universe into their ears for millennia. Have we lost them, and is it time to bring them back? The Emerald Tablet, a book of advice to kings, circa perhaps 3000 BC, said, "As above, so below. As within, so without." What its mystic author and many others since are saying is that the mysterious forces that create every aspect of life operate in a similar manner at every level. This includes the flower climbing out of the soil, the energy within a single atom, and the forces that drive human life.

It seems to me that we have lost the tradition of studying the mysteries of life and have not developed enough mystic teachers. Not studying the mystery of life is like not studying the nature of electricity and expecting to invent a power grid. Here's the definition of a mystic:

> *"A person who seeks by contemplation and self-surrender to obtain unity with or absorption into the Deity or the absolute, or who believes in the spiritual apprehension of truths that are beyond the intellect."*

What people sometimes study are the effects of the mysterious life force that are visible. But scientists today, and mystics before them who studied the nature of ultimate reality, have found patterns in this force, patterns that are the cause of the effects we see.

Since civilization began, leaders have worked with wise advisors who had deep understandings of these forces, and used these understandings to build frameworks for the foundation of their societies, many of whose accomplishments still defy our understanding today.

Who advises you? Are you open to sage advice or is it too threatening to your ego? No person has ever invented anything without the counsel of friends, so begin developing your own advisory board.

Don't Stop Paying Attention

When a cognitive framework starts to produce success, we see it as truth instead of an approximation. As we become attached to the power and success of the framework, we begin to ignore the wisdom we have found, and often throw it and those who have advised us out of our life (or out of the boardroom). We lose contact with the deeper realities whose changing currents affect our world, and find the once-powerful frameworks harmful. If you do not have a tradition of respect for the study of the nature of the universe, and don't seem to be listening to anyone, begin listening now.

Our frameworks have created powers that are capable of destroying our world, and wisdom often can't seem to get any press or an ear in the boardroom of corporations or governments.

Here's my question to you: How do you bring back the wise advisors of old (or call them what you will) and start to adjust your old operating frameworks before they destroy your life?

Inner Purpose: An Example of Wisdom

In Eckhart Tolle's book, *A New Earth*, he talks about the importance of reconciliation between your inner and outer purpose. He says,

> *"If you look within rather than only without, ... you discover that you have an inner and an outer purpose, and since you are a microcosmic reflection of the macrocosm, it follows that the universe too has an inner and outer purpose inseparable from yours."*

I have found that teams of leaders are attracted to each other, and to particular professions and businesses. Sometimes, this common outer purpose is a reflection of a deeper inner purpose. But often that deeper inner purpose, which can supercharge the outer purpose, is not always clear to each individual or the team. When each leader begins to discover his or her inner purpose or genius, the level of "acceptance, enjoyment, and enthusiasm," which Eckhart Tolle feels is an indicator of this alignment, goes up dramatically. Each leader then begins to see the synergy in the team, and creativity expands. The organizational culture becomes vibrant, people want to be part of it, and the marketplace finds that being connected to the business and its people is irresistible, because on some level they recognize the expression of wisdom.

> *"When something resonates to our purpose in life, when something resonates to a contribution that we want to make, when something resonates to a service that we want to perform, there is a solidity and a recognition that takes place within you. When you follow this resonance, this inner guidance, this experience, it becomes easier for you to recognize over time."*
> —**Lawerence Koh, President, International Diversified Products**

It takes courage to take the first step toward this state of being. It seems that we fear transcendence more than "the darkness." Our egos, fears, and the world tell us some of these leading-edge discoveries are crazy and dangerous dreams, but they are not crazy—it is our purpose to discover and manifest new realities. Imagine what our world would be like if every corporation, country, and community was an outward expression of true inner purpose and genius.

A Simple Example

I once interviewed a woman, whose name I have since forgotten, who is the CEO of an airport service. You park your car at their facility, and they take you to the terminal at the beginning of your trip and pick you up when you return. She started with one facility, and now has three centers around the Philadelphia airport.

When I asked her what contributed to her success, she said, "The people. When I interview, I look for people who smile easily." She explained that people like a friendly service when they travel, and that is why her venture is so popular. She matched the inner purpose of naturally friendly people with the outer purpose of her business. This is very similar to Lawrence Koh's story about the resonant tuning forks (see Chapter 1).

In her airport service business, the CEO attracted like people who resonated with the purpose of her business. You can do the same with your life.

PRACTICES and ACTIONS

As in the case of learning and developing any skill, there is no substitute for practice. I recommend the following.

1. We all have beliefs about reality. The key is to hold them lightly and use those beliefs as a platform for discovering new realities.

2. Build your knowledge around your desired career. Read everything. Remember, wisdom grows out of knowledge.

3. Spend time with those who are seeking their own wisdom and are willing to help you find yours. Sometimes others can see you better that you see yourself.

4. Work on your level of pattern recognition. Remember that knowledge is only a representation of reality. Knowledge points to truth, but the truth must still be discovered.

5. Learn to know the difference between the messages that come from your ego and those that are true insight.

Chapter 5

Use Intuition

Have you ever heard of a new product or concept and said, "I knew that," or "I thought of that years ago"? Have you ever had a bad feeling about someone and found out later they died or got into a serious accident. Have you ever called a friend, only to hear him state, "I was just about to call you"? We all have the ability to use our intuition. Many people question themselves and do not act on their intuition until it is too late, but great leaders have learned to use it. The key is recognizing the difference between true intuitive knowledge and simply fears or wild hopes.

5: Use Intuition

"Sometimes the feeling would last all the way to the end of the game, and when that happened I never cared who won ... If we lost, I'd still be as free and high as a sky hawk."

—William F. Russell, *Second Wind: The Memoirs of an Opinionated Man*

"Whenever I have gone against my intuition, I have regretted it."

—Don Ross, Chairman and CEO, New York Life

Photo: Sarah Clarehart

Every leader I interviewed for this book talked about the importance of intuition. In any endeavor, there is a correct course to set. As with a sailor who masters the relationship between the winds, which cannot be controlled, and the sails and rudder, which can, the right combination maximizes speed and targeting. In life or business, that course is based on the winds of change, competitive analysis, and the true differentiation of the product or service you might want to provide. A leader must be fully present in the reality of the moment to succeed, rather than being attached to his or her thoughts and beliefs about that reality that came from the past. Leaders must know the difference between the ego's hopes and fears, and true reality. This involves a deep understanding of the self and the flow of cause and effect. Leaders must learn to know and trust their intuition, which is like being "in the zone." You just know what to do in every moment, but it takes practice.

A Certain Knowing

Tony Bennett, in an interview with Piers Morgan on CNN, described the moment when he decided to become a singer at the age of 14. He was always encouraged to entertain his family with singing. He said, "I knew this is what I was meant to do." How did he know? He trusted and acted upon his intuition.

Tony went on to explain how he and Rosemary Clooney were in a singing contest. She came in first, and he came in second. He added, "As it should have been; she was a beautiful person." Later a talent scout spotted them both, and told Tony that he had a gift, but would need hard work and about seven years of practice to fully express that gift to an audience. Once we understand our natural genius, we tend to have the courage to act on our intuition with hard work and practice. Here's what

G. J. Hart, chairman and CEO of California Pizza Kitchen, said in a *New York Times* interview when asked about his leadership practices:

> *"I call them the six steps of leadership, surrounded by courage. Courage is an interesting one because any leadership role is about stepping out and having the courage to be different, because you have to be different to be a leader."*

It takes courage to ask for help. Tony Bennett went on to explain how he set himself up to be mentored by Frank Sinatra and many of the great singers who preceded him. Knowing that singing was his life purpose gave him the will and courage to accept feedback and commit to continuous learning around his gift.

Do you know what your natural gift is? If not, what are you doing to discover it? If you know the answer to this question, your life will be rich.

The Great Intelligence

An atom, the building block of matter, is about 99 percent space. The remaining parts are neutrons and protons, clustered at the center, and electrons that circle the center the way planets circle our sun. The neutrons, protons, and electrons are all spinning vortexes that are electrically charged. Each has what is called subatomic particles. The reason matter appears to be solid is that the spin forms a holographic effect, like the spokes on a bicycle when the wheel is spinning. You cannot put your hand through the spokes when the wheel is spinning. Atoms are always spinning, and they each have a different frequency, so you cannot walk through a wall.

Our universe is made up of formless space, which is 99 percent of existence, and yet seems to have its own intelligence. Science knows only the effect of this intelligence as it expresses itself in form. Mystics, philosophers, and the founders of the great spiritual practices would call this intelligence God. Therefore, as Jesus and others have said, "The kingdom of Heaven is within you." Each of us floats in, and is cradled by, this formless intelligence. That is why wise beings are always telling us to look within. The question is, how do we integrate this intelligence into our daily life? It comes through knowing and trusting our intuition. It is a certain feeling.

G. J. Hart uses his gut when he is interviewing new team members. He said:

> *"A lot of interviewing, quite frankly, is based on experience, gut, what makes sense, and what's in their eyes. What are they feeling? How will they react?"*

If you do the practices in this book, you will be able to determine whether your intuition comes from your inner knowing, or from your fears and wild hopes.

Connectivity

What if a communication network existed that worked without hardware, and was not limited by time and space? Would you be interested? In the ancient world, great ideas emerged at the same times in history on different continents, without any visible connectors. For example, the pyramids in Central and South America have an amazing similarity to those in China, and archaeologists wonder if there might have been some trans-Pacific sharing of designs or other ideas. They have not found any evidence of journeys or conduits, though Thor Heyerdahl's Kon-Tiki sail in the 1940s suggests that such ancient journeys were possible. Likewise, stone circles appeared all over Europe more than five thousand years ago without any real communication between cultures. If there is some sort of connectivity that we are just beginning to understand, it would follow that intuition maybe a way to benefit from that connectivity.

Birds of One Mind

In London in the 1940s birds suddenly learned how to peck the caps off of milk bottles to drink the cream that would rise to the top before pasteurization. This behavior spread quickly, and scientists are still trying to figure out how the birds communicated this skill to one another. Even the CIA is working on psychic abilities to predict events and find people. Today the desire for freedom and its immense benefits, seems to be swelling in the hearts and minds of people all over the world with the help of the Internet and social media. But are there other forces at work?

If there were a communication network that accounted for trends, inventions, and feelings of people around the world, business leaders would certainly be interested. Based on scientific studies of quantum physics, not only does this network exist, but it communicates outside of time and space. It sends out signals instantly, without the passage of time over any distance. This again goes to the article I mentioned in Chapter 4 by quantum physicist Antoine Suarez, who was quoted in an article in *Discover* magazine regarding a concept he calls "entanglement."

Know How it Feels

When I have asked people to describe how they feel when they experience being "in the zone," they offer words such as confident, at peace, exhilarated, powerful, graceful, and present. Some report a slow-motion effect as time slows. Kareem Abdul-Jabbar has stated how the five seconds he had to win the NBA championship with one shot seemed like five minutes to him. He felt relaxed, as if he had all the time in the world, yet he appeared to move like lightning to everyone else—the very definition of what I called "Integrative Presence" in my previous book. His creativity within these few precious seconds was nothing less than pure genius. He was integrating the skills he had learned over the years, his desire to make the shot, and the flow of the moment.

Your challenge is to begin to learn the difference between your thoughts, fears and fantasies, and be able to slip into "the zone" at will.

A Natural State of Mind

As I have experienced and studied athletes who are "in the zone," or exhibiting Integrative Presence, I have found that this state of mind, though not often reached, is a natural way of living. It seems we have lost touch with our true intuition. Ironically, the art of getting into this state of mind is letting go of what you think you know. You don't need to train yourself to experience Integrative Presence; you merely need to "let go." This state takes over your consciousness and supercharges your performance because it is in our nature to live this way.

Sports create highly charged environments. They are designed to bring out the best in people. But can this state be achieved outside of this arena? If these states of mind that seem to create superhuman results can be created in one area of life, certainly they could be created in others. Although the environment is particularly right for this kind of performance in sports, it is not beyond or separate from the "real world" in which we all operate.

What Is Genius?

In Roman mythology, genius was a "guardian deity or spirit that watched over each person from birth" and derived from a Latin word meaning "inborn nature." To unleash your genius, you need to stop resisting your spirit's advice and collaborate with the knowing that has been given to you.

As I define it, genius is collaboration with the natural flow that extends from the present, and from the knowledge, intention, and consciousness of an individual or group. It is achieved through Integrative Presence, which enables you to integrate all the realities of the flow of the moment while simultaneously combining them with the intention of your genius.

David Neagle, a business mentor and bestselling author of *The Millions Within*, said in a talk, *"Your true heart's desire is always projecting out into the world ... will you say yes or no to it?"* I believe that your heart's desire is always an expression of your genius. It is an expression of your purpose through connection with the divine. The challenge is to know the difference between the messages coming from your genius and your ego.

In his book, *Second Wind: The Memoirs of an Opinionated Man*, basketball star Bill Russell talks about the feeling of being in the zone:

"Sometimes the feeling would last all the way to the end of the game, and when that happened I never cared who won. I can honestly say that those few times were the only ones when I did not care ... On the five or ten occasions when the game ended at that special level, I literally did not care who had won. If we lost, I'd still be as free and high as a skyhawk."

Bill Russell and the Boston Celtics won eleven NBA championships in thirteen years.

How to Listen to Your Inner Compass

Cause and effect moves with or without you. The flows of cause and effect move events, stimulate ideas, and drive consumer wants and needs because everything is connected. This flow has a powerful momentum, and moves like the multidimensional currents in a powerful river. It moves forward with or without your conscious involvement. We are all connected to it even if we are not aware of our connection. The more you are consciously in sync with "the life force," the faster, more targeted, and powerful your actions become. Like an athlete in the zone, you are able to accelerate your performance with grace and ease.

Imagine how difficult life would be if you were not aware of these flows. (Many of us are not.) It would be like hiking through a wilderness fog without a compass. Even if you knew you needed to go north, you could not tell which way that was. You need an inner compass to navigate through the flows of cause and effect that influence every moment of your life—a way to understand where you are, and where the flow of history is going. But what is, and what is the practical use of, your inner compass?

What Is Your Inner Compass?

When I was working during the summer of 1987 as a leadership consultant to Don Ross, chairman and CEO of New York Life, many people came to me questioning his actions. He had asked the finance department to slowly move all investments out of the stock market into conservative instruments. This frustrated his investment team because the stock market was at an all-time high, and their competitors were using "high yield bonds" and stocks to create gains much greater than New York Life's. They wanted to play in the game, and Don Ross was telling them to step back.

Many people came to me, as Don's coach, to suggest I persuade him of the foolishness of his actions. I explained that I was his leadership coach and had little knowledge of the financial markets, but encouraged them to speak directly to Don. However, no matter how people pleaded, he would not change course. Several key players resigned and went to more "progressive" companies.

In October 1987, while I was on site at New York Life, the stock market crashed—the largest drop since the Great Depression. But New York Life had moved most of its investments out of the stock market and no longer held those high-yield instruments known later as "junk bonds." Don Ross was now considered a genius.

A week or so later, I asked Don how he knew to pull all of the company's investments out of the stock market three months before the crash. He said, "I just knew it couldn't last." Everyone in his world thought he was wrong, yet he had the wisdom and courage to do what he felt was right.

Knowing the Difference

When I pressed Don to tell me more, he explained that, as chairman and CEO, he was continuously bombarded with "experts" trying to convince him of completely different strategic directions. Each had incredible credentials and a good story, yet each recommended different strategies. The only tool he had to make the final decision was his instinct, or intuition. He said, "Whenever I have gone against my intuition, I have regretted it."

He further explained to me, "The key to wisdom is to know the difference between your wild hopes and fears and common sense, intuition, or true wisdom." They often seem the same, but they are not. There is a distinct difference in the feeling. One comes from the ego and insecurity, and the other from wisdom. Great leaders learn the difference and, given this knowledge, develop the courage to act quickly. Don had found ways to live in the present like an athlete in the zone, but with that easier, more sustainable feeling I call Integrative Presence—or at least he was able to find that state of mind when he needed insight. When I met with him over the years, he was often in the state of Integrative Presence. He was warm, yet seemed to be able to see through people. Always insightful, he moved with grace and ease.

The Courage to Act

All of the great leaders I have worked with know how to achieve Integrative Presence, even though they may not understand the nature of this state of mind. They have experienced being connected to something that supercharges their own knowledge. They speak reverently about this connection in private, but rarely talk about it to the press. It just seems too outside the norm for stockholders and the public.

Nevertheless, knowing and connecting to wisdom through Integrative Presence is essential for leaders in business today. Markets move quickly, often with little warning, and the wise leader can feel the moving currents. At each moment, like a surfer, the conscious leaders are so present that they take advantage of trends as they emerge. To create your own future, know the difference between your true intuition, your fears, and your hopes.

PRACTICES and ACTIONS

"Let the game come to you." —**Phil Jackson, NBA Head Coach and Guru**

1. Understand the difference between your intuition and the fears and hopes your ego sends to you. Practice using your intuition on simple things like the following:

- Guess who will win a sports match.
- Without a map or GPS, return to a place you have been to only once.
- Imagine what someone is going to say before they say it.

2. Write in your journal about times in your life when your intuition worked, including the times you ignored it and the times you followed it.

3. Learn to let go of your thoughts and clear your mind with activities such as these:

   - Meditation
   - Running
   - Cycling
   - Swimming
   - Dancing
   - Yoga
   - Weight-lifting
   - Deep relaxation

4. Remember that your thoughts are, at best, an approximation of reality, not reality itself.

5. Watch your thoughts rise and fall.

6. Become an objective observer of your thoughts.

7. Notice the repeating patterns of your thoughts.

8. Learn to laugh at yourself.

9. Practice noticing your thoughts and letting go of them.

"Whenever I have gone against my intuition, I have regretted it."

—**Don Ross, Chairman and CEO, New York Life**

PART THREE:

PAINT COMPELLING PICTURES

Chapter 6

Conceive the Future

You cannot create something you cannot conceive. It is important for you to have a clear, compelling, multisensory picture of your future, project, or strategy. To get other people to help create your future, start with ten people who also can recognize your vision, and then work until there are thousands. If you are a leader, make sure everyone in your company or organization can conceive this picture.

Photo: Sarah Clarehart

6: **Conceive the Future**

"*Dream big. What's the world of possibilities for yourself and for your organization? You have to be able to say, 'Here's where I want to go.' It's not that you'll ever necessarily get there, but if you don't dream, you'll never even get started.*"

—G. J. Hart, Chairman and CEO, California Pizza Kitchen

"*A big portion of excitement and enthusiasm comes from leadership. It is about understanding where one is going.*"

—Linda LoRe, CEO, Frederick's of Hollywood

"*A true visionary is the one who can hold a vision when everybody else is giving up on visions.*"

—Tony LoRe, CEO, Youth Mentoring Connection

Photo: Sarah Clarehart

The tribe gathers around a raging fire under the full moon. The warriors enact the coming hunt by the light of the fire. Each step in the strategy plays out in a magical dance, while the elders and the council chief watch and chant to the drums. All are gathered to prepare for the last hunt before the herd moves south for the winter. The tribe's survival depends on the hunt's success.

The next morning the warriors move out before dawn and silently approach the herd, surrounding them as planned, galloping in from all sides on the leader's signal.

The hunt begins at sunrise and ends with celebration around the fire, with stories of danger and glory during the hunt. The young men watch and learn, while the elders give out acknowledgment to the warriors, and later will pass some words of caution in private. It is important who speaks and what lessons they share. At that time, as for thousands of years, the tribe's wisdom is passed down through storytelling.

It is no wonder, when a good storyteller begins, that the occasion feels important. Some wisdom is about to be passed along. In fact, before the written word, all wisdom was passed on in the oral tradition. In Native America traditions, the warriors painted a compelling picture of success to prepare for the hunt, sharing stories and wisdom from the hunt itself. By painting compelling pictures, the tribe's leaders motivated and focused the tribe, especially its young warriors, who were still learning.

You Cannot Create Something You Cannot Conceive

When a leader knows the answer or the right course, he or she must be able to conceive and communicate the opportunity and understand how the team can capture it. Until this team can see, feel, and hear the calling of the opportunity that present reality represents, it cannot truly follow. Without this clear picture, each team member will create his or her own vision of the future, if at all, causing friction and slowing the team's overall progress.

The leader's presence and authentic commitment to the mission draws followers within the company and in the marketplace. The more clearly the future state is pictured, the easier it is to create. Without a clear vision of the future in the mind of each leader, chaos will ensue.

> *"I came in as president of Shakey's Pizza. This was a brand that had been a leader of its category years and years ago, but now had declining sales for well over a decade. It was one of those brands that looked like it was rolling into the morgue. First I met with my team, and we went out and looked at the competition. Everyone looked at the products, looked at the experience of the competitors. Then we met back at Shakey's, and we said, 'All right, here is the Shakey's experience; how does it compare with the competition?'"* —**Tim Pulido, President and CEO of Campero USA and Pollo Campero International**

Tim went on to explain how they remodeled several stores, tested the reactions of customers, and fine-tuned the environment and the pizzas themselves until customer traffic and sales went up. They tested their concepts through model stores, which became compelling pictures for the future, "pictures" that management and staff could walk into to see what the company's future could look like. Once they understood the positive reaction customers where having, they rolled the remodel out to all their stores. Tim had the courage to acknowledge reality and respond with a compelling picture for the future.

> *"When we put all those things together—uniforms, products, remodeled stores, improved games, and everything else—suddenly the total package came together. Our restaurants were seeing 15 to 20 percent growth."* —**Tim Pulido, President and CEO of Campero USA and Pollo Compero International**

In whatever you are trying to create, what is your compelling picture? Maybe you cannot build a model store for people to walk into, but you must find ways to portray a compelling picture of a future state. People have a deep fear of the unknown. As children, when we walked into a dark room looking for a light switch, our minds imagined monsters, not pots of gold or ponies. As adults, we still do not like walking into that dark room.

As leaders, you must light the way forward so people can see themselves as part of your picture. If your team, customers, and the market do not already feel that way, then it time to communicate your vision more effectively.

Fast Forward to Today

An excellent example of a compelling picture of the future happened at a seven-day conference at California Pizza Kitchen (CPK), at which they held their second annual awards banquet. The event was led by G. J. Hart, who had been CEO of CPK for eighteen months. He faced the daunting task of leading the change of a corporate culture that had allowed CPK to fall way behind its competitors. Every moment during those seven days painted a rich picture of what the future could become if everyone was "all in." The conference was a masterpiece of theater and inspiration, complete with campfires and dancing.

The CPK conference was very much like the tribe preparing for the hunt. The importance of who was speaking and the stories they told passed the wisdom on in a similar manner. Successful warriors received praise for honoring the tribe. They told stories about how they won while the young leaders and their families watched—this time on digital screens instead of around the fire.

Every award given at the banquet carried an authentic human story that was a living example of the future G. J. wanted to create. He and his wife, Michelle, rolled out programs they called "Inspired Acts" to seven needy community service organizations that surrounded the hotel where CPK held its conference.

Gifts of refrigerators, ovens, and other important equipment for kitchens and other needs were sent in advance by Michelle and her team. For a full day, 600 people spread among community-service organizations and helped them with gardens, painting, building things they needed, resodding a recreational facility, and clearing vines from trees in a park. Vendors, managers, leaders, their significant others, and even hotel staff spent a day doing "Inspired Acts." The whole tribe worked together to help those in need. Learn more about CPK's Inspired Acts initiative here.

The "Inspired Acts" created a purpose for the enterprise that is beyond making money. It made the team members feel like they were part of something greater that the corporation and themselves. Many of the leaders in this business, including the CEO, come up from humble means. They all have a feeling of compassion for those who struggle to get ahead. A great sense of loyalty has been engendered. Additionally, these kinds of "Inspired Acts" are part of CPKs community outreach where each restaurant is located.

Three of the primal human needs were addressed masterfully in this conference.

1. The fear of the unknown, which the compelling pictures of the future addressed.
2. The need to be part of, and not banished, from the tribe, which at one time meant certain death.
3. The desire to be part of something greater than ourselves.

All were handled in a natural and authentic manner.

Passionate Storytelling

A group of leaders telling stories is still more powerful than the written word. Over the years of leading change, I have found that simple stories that create insight are the most effective way to change people's beliefs and behaviors. A single authentic story can change corporations, people, and countries.

G. J. is skilled at aligning CPK's business mission with a deep sense of purpose through his stories. He believes in and role-models a heartfelt leadership. From this deeply caring place, he is able to inspire people to go above and beyond the call of duty, and the CPK family expects nothing less. G. J. knows that with the right coaching, people are capable of exceeding their own expectations.

G. J. makes it clear by what he says and does that his company's highest calling is for its people to serve one another, the communities in which CPK does business, and humanity itself. This passion rings in his tone of voice, and shines in his eyes. He is always striving to invent a better future for everyone around him.

How Passionate Are You?

G. J. Hart created a powerful example with his storytelling about the heroes who are acknowledged throughout CPK's awards banquet, and has influenced hundreds of his leaders. As he described how each made a difference in a customer's, employee's or a community member's life, people in the room were inspired to do the same. Tears of joy were shed throughout the conference.

If you do not have hundreds of leaders following you, job one will be to find the first person in your life who can tell your story about the future you are trying to invent. Then find nine more.

You might be thinking "Who would care about my story?" Well, remember what G. J. said: *"Dream big. What's the world of possibilities for yourself and for your organization?"* Enroll those who believe in you in your dream, and give them stories they can tell to their friends. Show passion and courage. Get hundreds of people involved in inventing your future. Most of the successful CEOs I've worked with have hundreds or even thousands of people who can tell their story.

Rosemary's Dream

Rosemary Cullinan, the restauranteur I introduced in Chapter 1, was a school teacher. She also waited on tables in a restaurant while she was teaching so she could earn extra money, and found that she enjoyed the social interaction. When her teaching position was eliminated, she started working as a full-time waitress. She loved the business, and always wanted to own her own restaurant.

On the day she said yes to her dream, she had looked at Craigslist and saw that a little restaurant called the Peninsula Cafe was for sale. She told me, "At that moment I knew!" She went to this restaurant in our neighborhood in Long Beach, California, and made a purchase offer on the spot. She had a compelling picture in her mind of what it would look like. She loves people, which is very important in the restaurant business, but knew very little about the details of running such an establishment.

Rosemary greeted everyone who entered with genuine interest and caring. She remembered their names and created a wonderful atmosphere. When my wife Bonnie and I were out of town and did not go to the cafe for a while, our neighbors would ask, "Where were you?" They did this because Rosemary created a compelling picture of a community-gathering place. The entire community recruited neighbors to come and dine together.

The neighborhood supported her success. Not only did local residents come regularly, and bring their friends; they also helped her in times of trouble. When she had difficulty with other neighbors who complained about the noise that echoed through the alley from patio dining late at night, she formed an action committee to address the complaints. Additionally, because she had put her life savings into this venture and did not know how to keep her books, some neighbors gave her a loan and sent her to school to learn accounting and other restaurant managing skills.

Rosemary made the Peninsula Cafe into a place to connect with her, her staff, and our neighbors.

One day the first Sysco Restaurant Supply truck arrived very late, after Rosemary had gone home. One of the neighbors noticed, approached the driver and said, "Wait, I will call her on my cell phone and she will be right over." The driver later said, "I have never seen anything like this." This is connecting with your guests. It creates loyalty and success ... and it is the right thing to do.

Rosemary said to me,

> *"A business is like a marriage. You have got to love it, and I am in love with my business. It is sexy to me and it is not hard. I am always inspired to do better. I love sitting at home going through cookbooks and creating the Saturday night dinner. I look forward to it every week."*

You can sure tell when you walk into the cafe, when you might find her rolling dough for an apple pie. Ask yourself: When people approach you do they see how inspired you are? Is it a pleasure being around you, or your business? Can people feel that you love what you are doing, which we talked about in Chapter 1, "Become Your Calling"? You are the most important part of the compelling picture.

Rosemary's Lessons

Rosemary's story is full of many of the practices we have covered thus far. What can we discover about inventing the future from her story?

- **Know Yourself:** When she started waiting on people in the summers, Rosemary found her natural gift for being in service to people.

- **Know When You Know:** Rosemary had a knowing that kept whispering to her much of her life. This included a feeling for people, and a creative streak she expressed as an English literature teacher. Each day on the restaurant's chalk board, she wrote a quote about life.

- **Create Compelling Pictures:** With the success from being in service to people as a waitress in the summers, her dream emerged in her heart. She could see herself running this special gathering place.

- **Build Commitment:** When the opportunity to buy her own restaurant came, Rosemary acted with commitment and courage, and built commitment to her dream in the neighborhood by getting input from the neighbors, and describing her vision.

- **Respond to Reality:** Rosemary responded to reality when some of neighbors were blocking her, and in response to many other unforeseen issues. She realized she did not know enough about accounting, and asked one of her loyal customers for help.

- **Inner Stillness:** Because she was living her dream, even though she spent all her life savings, Rosemary displayed an inner stillness that gave her guests and staff confidence in her business.

This is, of course, a true story based on my own experience. It's important for leaders of both large and small businesses to tell compelling stories like this one. As you start to develop stories that illustrate the future you want to create for yourself, remember to build commitment by painting real and compelling pictures of the opportunity your business or new career might represent to people in your life.

Remember that just as the CEO of California Pizza Kitchen and the owner of a small café must tell compelling stories to get their workers committed to the new way, so you have to do the same with people in your life. But first you must understand your natural gifts and skills that will contribute to the future you want to invent.

Making It Personal

The stories of big and small businesses also apply on the personal level. John O. Brown is a forty-year-old who found himself doing a job that was not working out for him. He asked me if I could coach him through the process of inventing his future. Of course, we started with knowing himself, his natural genius, and the opportunities that best suited those gifts. The first step was a process for letting go of thoughts that blocked his genius. We worked until he was certain about his natural gifts. Then we targeted careers that fit those gifts. Following that, we wrote a simple summary of those skills and posted them on his LinkedIn profile. Here it is:

Bring Out People's Best with Collaboration

Having worked with all types of individuals over the last twenty years—creative types, artists, geeks, technologists, engineers, executives, and bean counters—I have learned to organize diverse people into effective teams. I always look for the best in coworkers and clients to deliver results far beyond their own expectations.

During my years in the entertainment industry and real estate development, I found that collaboration helps create empowerment and ideas that lead to more long-lasting and effective solutions. Taking the time to listen to clients and people at all levels in my organizations is key to understanding how to achieve, manage, and exceed their expectations.

Develop Road Maps for People to Follow

Using my ability to visualize patterns and procedures that support desired outcomes, I have set up project responsibilities and goals. Learning from mentors, I have discovered a methodology that breaks down any project into little goals that sync with each person's best skills. Together we establish clear responsibilities for individuals and team accountability for hitting targets.

This skill has been important to my work with highly creative people who like control over their work but have a hard time seeing how it fits into the overall team effort.

Inspire and Lead People to Exceed Expectations

It has always been my nature to find a better way. Since my core skills are leadership and management, I have found ways to inspire and organize teams around business missions. It is my experience that teams have few limitations to what they can achieve when they are motivated and organized in a logical manner.

I find out what motivates each individual and reward them in ways that inspire each person to take pride in exceeding his or her own expectations. My teams celebrate small and large successes, and do a post-action debrief every time we fall short to learn from our mistakes.

John is now preparing one or two stories from his life that paint a compelling picture of each of his skills and can be told in an interview, or to the people in his life that are committed to his success—first ten people, then twenty, until he has a strong brand in his community and on LinkedIn.

His next assignment is to join LinkedIn groups that are formed with people in John's chosen field, and join in the conversations with them, fitting his stories into the dialog. In fact, he is preparing a series of short stories and statements that tell the narrative in a personal way. When he has written these narratives, he and I will fine-tune them until he has six months of posts ready. He will then post one or two a week.

As he interviews, networks, or just discusses with friends his vision for the future and what he wants to create for himself, these stories will start to become part of what people talk about. At some point in time, someone will know someone who needs the skills and passion that John naturally brings.

PRACTICES and ACTIONS

Create your own story and paint a compelling picture. In today's world a story should last no more than three minutes, reveal personal insight, and be totally authentic. Your story must be relevant to issues at hand, and, so it can be retold, easily remembered, and repeated. Your story should begin with, "I would like to tell you a story about an event that changed my level of understanding, or life." To be effective, its three stages should follow these guidelines:

- **Beginning:** Describe the problem you faced, and the events that led to your insight. This stage ends with a pivot point, where it is clear something had to change.

- **Middle:** Tell people what you did differently, and, most important, the insight you had about yourself as a result. Describe the moment of epiphany.

- **Ending:** Explain the value, results, and how your life is now different. This section should be full of passion, gratitude, and wonder, demonstrating a commitment that reflects how you will act differently in the future.

These steps should have drama, be entertaining, and have a sudden level of insight that may not have been obvious from the beginning.

Chapter 7:

Create High-Impact Statements

As you begin to develop your own narrative—painting that compelling picture to get people on board with your vision—you can integrate proven practices into your methodology. Creating compelling and realistic statements will be key to your success.

7: Create High-Imact Statements

"Your commitment to cleaning up everything that does not support that compelling picture is important. When you have it right, and know it, you want new principles, and a different level of commitment."

—Tim Pulido, President and CEO, Campero USA and Pollo Campero International

The Rule of Three

Many executives and successful people in general have discovered what is called the rule of three. There are always three of something:

1. Three men walking into a bar
2. Three little pigs
3. The three wise men of the Bible

Why does this happen? Studies have shown that the human brain can best comprehend and remember three things, concepts, or reasons at any given time. There are many books and papers written about this topic.

The most powerful effect from this rule is achieved when the first two points lead to the third state. This layered effect creates insight. Just as a man and a woman create a third being, so should the structure of your communications rely on two important points that lead to a third. This should not be just a list, but a dynamic combination.

For example:

1. You know yourself.
2. Because you know yourself, your response to any problem will be obvious.
3. Then you can act with certainty.

When my partners and I built our consulting firm, our informal vision was "We are the McKinsey of leadership." In conceiving this vision statement, we combined two seemingly opposite types of firms, one known as the go-to consultants for business strategy and the other striving to become the go-to consultants for organizational leadership. The third point was implied: to provide a roadmap for the new leadership future. It is a powerfully implied future state.

Similarly, the phrase "Invent Your Future" suggests that if you invent it you will be in control of your destiny. It also implies that if you do not invent your future, someone else might. Just three words.

John F. Kennedy said, "Ask not what your country can do for you; ask what you can do for your country." The third state here is powerfully implied: doing something for your country is just the right thing to do.

Ronald Reagan, having been an actor, always had a sense of the setting. When he gave his famous speech at the Brandenburg Gate in Berlin, he said, "Mr. Gorbachev, tear down this wall." A divided Berlin was the center of the Cold War. He used the visual to create the third and desired state. You could almost see the wall coming down and people flooding over it as he spoke.

Tim Pulido's Four Cs

Tim Pulido uses four notions, but as you look at it, the fourth concept is actually the combination of the first three. Here's what he says:

> *"I use what I call the four Cs: clarity, commitment, courage, and character. Clarity is my way of acknowledging reality with brutal facts. As you confront those, they lead you to what you need to do in any situation. When you can look at them objectively, they lead you to knowing the answer to any problem or strategy. Clarity for me is what I call strategic clarity or business clarity—you know clearly what you want to be, and how you are going to get there. The compelling picture is then in place.*

> *"Your commitment to cleaning up everything that does not support that compelling picture is important. When you have it right, and know it, you want new principles, and a different level of commitment. You clean out the old and bring in the new, but often people have difficulty letting go of the old. It takes a high level of commitment."*

Henry Walker's Picture

Most leaders focus on what they want people to do but leave out the "why" and "how." Once someone understands why any action or strategy is important they are empowered. They still may need training in how, but as circumstances change they will be able to adjust how to manifest the why without moment-to-moment guidance.

Henry Walker, President of Farmers and Merchants Bank, had just met with his staff to go over a strategic plan for doubling earnings growth. He also painted a rich picture of the importance of customer service that is full of why, what, and how. To be sure this could be translated into something every employee would remember, he told his leaders how to translate that vision into everyday disciplines for the people on the front lines. Again he gave each employee three things to remember:

1. Smile—we want to create a friendly environment in our banks.
2. Get to know customers by name and understand what their lives are about.
3. Cross-sell the bank's different products to meet the needs of their lives.

As Henry says:

> *"To be sure that our employees are committed and stay committed, I have people 'mystery shop' the branches to be sure these behaviors are in place. If not, we take those falling short through a review process that helps them build commitment and effective practices. No matter how grand your vision for the future, you have to discover and manifest how that vision translates into day-to-day disciplines and actions. We work on building commitment every day."*

Translating Compelling Pictures Into Simple Practices

You cannot create something you cannot conceive, and some people have a limited ability to accomplish the latter. So you have to help them see their part. The stonecutter may not see the picture of the entire cathedral, but has a clear picture of the wall he is building. Some hold the bigger picture and others hold part of that picture.

In your life you have to be sure that people around you know what to do to support your vision. It is not enough to tell them the big picture. They need a picture of what they can do to help.

For example, when my business consulting clients are happy with my work and want to refer me, I say the following, "Please do not try and sell the services I provided for you. They may need something entirely different. Just tell them that I helped you succeed, and recommend that they meet with me. It should be an interesting meeting." This gives them a simple picture of how they can help me, but is not asking them to sell for me.

Target ten people in your life and build a clear picture of how they can help you. After ten, enlist ten more, and then another ten, until you have hundreds of people who can promote you.

Jack Welch Said

Senn Delaney leadership was waiting in a conference room to interview Jack Welch for a book we were writing called *Leadership in the 21st Century*. He came into the room and apologized for being late, and then explained that he had felt a little ill after his speech. As he put it, "I give two or three speeches a week and I always say the same three things. I get sick of hearing myself say them, but I know if I do not repeat these things, then GE will get off track."

Here are some of the things that Jack has often said:

> *"Number one, cash is king … number two, communicate … number three, buy or bury the competition."*

> *"Control your own destiny or someone else will."*

> *"Willingness to change is a strength, even if it means plunging part of the company into total confusion for a while."*

"Good business leaders create a vision, articulate the vision, passionately own the vision, and relentlessly drive it to completion."

Jack led General Electric to become the most profitable company in the world, which was no easy task. He had a knack for communicating a power statement.

Repeat Key Understandings

Jack knew from experience that key messages need to be repeated to take hold. I had read a study done a little over twenty years ago on cognitive skills. Covering Europe and North America, it found that 85 percent of people could not hold a mildly complex cognitive framework in their heads for more than two weeks. Within the two weeks their cognitive retention resembles a bell curve. Only 10 percent could hold a mildly complex framework indefinitely, but could not do "what ifs." Only 5 percent could hold and play with mildly complex cognitive frameworks and see the consequences of changes within them.

This is why it is very important to repeat key understandings about any endeavor for which you need the support of others. Keep the understandings simple, and never have more than three. It is much easier to hold three things in your mind than four or beyond. The brain just seems to be structured this way. For example, I help you unleash genius, and invent your future with the following components:

1. Leadership development
2. Team-building
3. Fast-break execution

Here I used three statements, outside of my being an author, which describes exactly what I do. If each item in the three is related to the others, the mind can more easily digest this framework, and then be ready for the next. But it will be important to repeat these understandings often, and in different ways.

This approach finds expression in everything I do. My mission is clear to me and in the minds of friends and supporters. It is a compelling picture of what you can expect if you work with me or invite a friend to meet me.

Once you know what you want to invent, create a targeted and memorable picture in people's minds.

PRACTICES and ACTIONS

"I believe that intention works to create the future when you are connected to your purpose, or who you are meant to be."

—**Matt Witte, Managing Partner, Marwit Investment Management LLC**

1. Write down in your journal all of the things you love to do. Capture each of these joyful acts, no matter how trivial. Understand the nature of your feelings when you are doing these activities.

2. Spend time reflecting on the commonalities in all the things you love to do, not just the activities but the feeling and skill underneath them.

3. Start to create a narrative linking together all the skills that you have used when you are doing things you love. In this manner you and those who can support you can visualize your essential gifts.

4. As you look for a career, a business you might want to start, or a product you might launch, observe how the narrative of the things you love to do fits into three key drivers of success.

5. If you have not distilled your natural genius from the work in Chapter 1, go back and finish that work, before you begin this.

6. Express your gifts, or natural genius, in a way that presents them in a unique, practical, and authentic way.

7. Develop a compelling picture of the future you would like to invent, expressed in short impactful combinations of three, like the examples in this chapter.

8. Develop a series of personal stories about the "why, what, and how" of similar futures you were part of inventing.

9. Start telling your stories to family and friends, building a team of supporters. Set goals for how many people you would like to understand who you are, or what you want to do.

10. After mastering the preceding, convert your narrative into a social networking process and context.

Remember, you cannot create something you cannot conceive, nor can others help you if you cannot paint a picture of your dream and show how others can help. This process works for building a new company, launching a new product, creating a new organizational culture, landing a job, or finding a new calling.

There is no substitute for practice!

PART FOUR:

BUILD
COMMITMENT

Chapter 8:

Inspire Everyone

Positive motivation works much better than fear. When we are fearful, we fall into a defense mode called "fight or flight." When that occurs, our blood runs from our brain and internal organs to our arms and legs so we can run or fight. If someone attacks us, all we will be able to see is the gun or knife he or she is holding. The result is a narrow consciousness. Creativity and commitment requires a wide consciousness that can see into the future.

"Ask yourself, on a scale of one to ten, have you done everything possible to achieve your goal? This will tell you how committed you really are."
—Lloyd Wallis, President, Rubbercraft

"I never paid attention to the naysayers. I mean, I heard what they were saying, I noticed it, but I didn't let that get in my way, because fear is the most crippling emotion that an organization can have, or a person can have."
—Linda LoRe, CEO, Frederick's of Hollywood

"They shot my friends too. They thought that the bullets would silence us. But they failed, and out of that silence came thousands of voices."
—Malala Yousafzai, at the United Nations after previously being shot in the head at point-blank range for standing up for women's right to education

"We work on building commitment every day."
—Henry Walker, President, Farmers and Merchants Bank

Photo: Sarah Clarehart

Casey Sheahan, President and CEO of Patagonia, said this to me during our interviews for this book:

> *"Inspiration has to start with you. If you don't believe that you can affect positive change, then it won't happen. But if you can inspire people, as opposed to motivating them with fear, then you know there is a better outcome possible … I think you can really light people up. You can light your customers up, and you can light your manufacturers up too. When people are inspired, you get a better result, working conditions, and high-quality products. It is a priority for us."*

Inspire Total Commitment

At the age of sixteen, Pakistan's Malala Yousafzai was shot in the head at point-blank range by the Taliban for standing up for women's right to education. On July 12, 2013, with the Taliban vowing to kill her, she stood before the United Nations in New York City and said the following, speaking out for the first time since she was attacked:

> *"Let us pick up our books and pens. They are our most powerful weapons. One child, one teacher, one pen, and one book can change the world. Education is the only solution."*

Wearing her usual pink head scarf, Yousafzai told U.N. Secretary-General Ban Ki-moon and nearly 1,000 students attending an International Youth Assembly that education was the only way to improve lives.

> *"They shot my friends too. They thought that the bullets would silence us. But they failed, and out of that silence came thousands of voices. The terrorists thought they would change my aims and stop my ambitions, but*

nothing changed in my life except this: weakness, fear, and hopelessness died. Strength, power, and courage was born."

Reuters reported that she wore a white shawl draped around her shoulders that had belonged to former Pakistani Prime Minister Benazir Bhutto, who was assassinated during a 2007 election rally weeks after she returned to Pakistan from years in self-imposed exile.

This is total commitment, fueled by enormous courage. The Taliban has said that they will find her and kill her next time.

Anything I could say about my own struggles with commitment is dwarfed by her example, but I am going to share my experience anyway. I took a personal development course more than thirty years ago, and the one point that stood out for me was the importance of keeping my commitments. When we break our commitments to others, over time we lose their trust, and that is hard to regain. When we break our commitments to ourselves, we lose trust in ourselves, and that too is hard to regain.

At this personal development course we had an assignment for one week to not break any commitments we made to ourselves. Not even the smallest thing, such as deciding to take a walk and then not doing it.

Try this for yourself, but do not say you are going to run sixty miles this week. Just observe the normal things you do, and be sure you keep every commitment you make to yourself and others. Then, at the end of the week, notice how your energy level is different. When I did this my energy doubled. From that moment on, I have kept all the commitments I have made to myself and others. Try this exercise for yourself. You will be amazed.

I am always on time to meetings and events because I wish to maintain my own level of commitment to myself.

Imagine the commitment it took for Malala to stand up for women's education in the face of serious death threats.

Anything I am willing to commit to is worth one hundred percent of my energy and focus. I always take Lloyd Wallis's advice and ask myself how committed I am on a scale of one to ten.

Linda LoRe came to Frederick's of Hollywood from Giorgio Beverly Hills, finding a broken and sad organizational culture. As she put it,

> *"There were 1,800 employees, and they were good people. They had talents. They had skills, but they were very broken-spirited."*

As CEO she had seen the direct opposite at Giorgio Beverly Hills, where everyone was strong, powerful, and committed to begin with.

> *"There was something inside me, because I had just come from an organization that worked. It flew so high and so fast, and it was a wonderful experience with Giorgio Beverly Hills. It just grew and, wow, I loved it. It was so exciting. I thought I had to bring just a portion of that excitement and enthusiasm, combined in a cohesiveness that is in Giorgio Beverly Hills. I said to myself, 'I'll try to capture that capability in this new organization to help people. And if I can do that, it will really be an exciting thing'."*

The art of being a leader is to challenge teams to face their fears and change their habits. The same is true for each of us. We have to challenge ourselves and overcome our fears. A book I've never read, because the title says it all, is Susan Jeffers' *Feel the Fear and Do It Anyway*. Courage is not the lack of fear, it is overcoming our fears. What prevents most people from commitment is a fear of the unknown and a fear of being wrong.

No one likes to walk into a dark room. We have to light the darkness of the unknown with our vision for the future. To move forward, we must paint a picture of a new reality to give ourselves the confidence to do so. The clearer and more compelling that picture of our future state becomes, the more committed we become. The same is true for the people you lead, the marketplace, and your customers.

Human beings are creatures of habit. We each develop distinct behaviors and routines, and while certain tactics may motivate employees in the short term, reverting back to old habits is nearly inevitable. Also, especially amid today's economic and political climate, an inherent mistrust of leadership has developed in the psyche of many Americans—making it harder than ever for a leader to gain and keep the trust needed to develop a truly cohesive team.

To management and executive teams, corporate goals are typically numbers—we need to make money, score points, defeat the competition. That is like a coach demanding that a team has to score more points, but not coaching the team on how to score.

What many leaders struggle to convey is a clear picture of how to score points. To commit to a vision, people need to visualize and relate to the mission in their hearts and minds. Money is often the outcome of the mission, just as scoring points is the outcome of a well-trained basketball team committed to a championship. A clear and compelling picture of "why, what, and how" can earn trust and inspire a team to incredible levels of commitment. The problem is often that leadership presents only numbers, not picturable visions.

Communicate your mission in a clear and concise way. Many higher-level business leaders use fear as a means to motivate their team to work faster to reach the mission. For example, they may say, "We will lose money if this task isn't completed." This is a strategy that simply does not work. Minds shut down, and consciousness is narrowed when individuals are put under that pressure. I always recommend that leaders instead build a strong culture within their team, using hopeful and positive messaging to expand consciousness and make team members feel like they belong.

All living things have the urge to grow. If I did not cut back my garden it would overgrow everything. People are the same, know it or not. A statement that describes the strategic window of opportunity for growth is much more powerful. It inspires growth and winning while challenging everyone to bring out their best. If a leader does not insist on professional and personal growth, and provide inspiration around the possibility the organizational culture will stagnate. Through developing a positive expanding corporate culture, team members will feel that they are working toward something "bigger than themselves," transcend their habits, and become committed to the organization's success. That creates real commitment.

Insist that you and your teams continually learn and grow. A company can grow only as fast as its people. If a leader can create an environment where learning is prized above all, team members will become attached to this dynamic environment, and will feel supported and appreciated—with employee retention becoming a nonissue.

When I was coaching the CEO of StarKist Foods, he said that he did not blame his people for his mistakes, but rather looked at the weaknesses of his team as attributable to his own failure to ensure that each employee was able to learn how to meet and exceed goals. His positivity created a team that trusted its leader and felt compelled to learn more, be better, and consistently achieve goals.

Being in a highly accountable organization committed to a mission fills a primal need of all humans. We all are more committed when we feel we are part of something bigger than ourselves and connected to others. Leaders can leverage this primal need by making all team members feel like they are part of a group where all individuals are accountable to one another, establishing a strong camaraderie.

How can you do this? I recommend taking employees outside of the office for team-building events—engaging in activities such as inviting them and their families to a sporting or cultural event, grabbing dinner after work, or even taking the team on a weekend retreat. Team members like the perks of these activities, but more important, consistent team-building forces the group to perform in a highly engaged environment, which translates to enhanced team playing back at the office.

The glue that holds a team together is appreciation, so make sure that you show yours. Many business leaders think handing an employee a paycheck or not firing an individual is enough. Giving recognition to your team members is crucial to establishing a trusting, inspired environment that builds commitment. Take time in meetings or outside of work to point out individual successes—and not just by saying "good job," but really asking questions to keep the team engaged. For example, you could ask questions such as "What was your strategy behind that decision?" or "How will you continue to be successful with this project?" By touting individual success, acknowledging team members, and engaging in conversation that shows true appreciation, peers will grow more dedicated to reaching their personal and team goals.

Implementing these strategies in your workplace will make your teams stronger, more successful, and more trusting in your leadership capabilities. By inspiring team members individually, and making them feel part of a group, your company will reap consistent business rewards for many years to come.

The same is true as we build our lives. Having teams of friends inspired by your leadership and missions will inspire a level of commitment to support you and your efforts. Ask yourself, are you acting as though you are the CEO of your life? Are you inspired and committed to your work, family, and community? You will experience multiple benefits by inspiring yourself first, and then others.

PRACTICES and ACTIONS

As Lloyd Wallis said, "Ask yourself, on a scale of one to ten, have you done everything possible to achieve your goal? This will tell you how committed you really are." Here are a few questions to test your level of commitment.

1. How often to you hesitate or pull back? It is natural to hesitate a little, but if you do it frequently, perhaps you have not done enough to create certainty.

2. Share your commitment with friends and see how they react. Your level of commitment will inspire theirs. If it does not inspire others, they will ask questions that indicate they are worried about you walking off a cliff.

3. If you are truly committed, you will automatically see routes to your commitment opening up in front of you.

4. If you are truly committed, all manner of ideas will flood into your consciousness, and the challenge will be to pick the best ideas, instead of struggling just to come up with them.

5. If you or someone following you does not pass the preceding tests, go back to the tasks of "knowing yourself," "knowing when you know," and looking deep and building a "compelling picture" that develops your commitment.

Chapter 9:

See and Feel Possibility

No matter how distant the goal, being able to see the possibility of a better way builds commitment. As I suggest in the Practices and Actions section of Chapter 8, if ideas and opportunities are not flooding into your consciousness, you are probably not truly committed. If going after your goal is draining your energy instead of energizing you, you're probably feeling a fear of being wrong or failing. When you are inventing a new future there is always fear of the unknown. To keep on target, you must be able to see and feel the possibility to overcome fears.

"We are all brought into this life with a noble, beautiful purpose. We are here for a reason. We each have a gift, and it is our job to find that gift. This is why we don't tell kids to change. In fact, I correct them when they say, 'I'm gonna change.' I say, 'I don't want you to change, I want you to become more of who you are.'"

—Tony LoRe, CEO, Youth Mentoring Connection

"A big portion of excitement and enthusiasm comes from leadership. It is about understanding where one is going."

—Linda LoRe, CEO, Frederick's of Hollywood

Photo: Sarah Clarehart

Bill McGinnis, CEO of National Technical Systems, an aerospace testing and certification company, explains how having his team help to build the picture of the future has created possibility and commitment.

> "Having my team be part of painting the picture, rather than simply giving them targets, is why it became so compelling to them and the market. Once they knew what they needed to do, and what was in it for them, they started executing with a velocity that was amazing. When we got that committed, we thought we could do anything. It's crazy. We actually did. We actually went from a company that was going backwards, certainly retracting, to a company that turned around to be, in our space, one of the fastest growing firms compared to our competitors."

Ask yourself: Are you involving people around you in creating the picture of the future you want to envision?

Is Our Need to "Be Right" a Curse?

It seems to me our need to "be right" is a blessing and a curse. When ancient people lived in tribes, it was even more important. If a tribe did not gather and hunt enough food to survive the winter, everyone would perish. Today it is important to "be right" about our savings, preparing for retirement, and having a job that supports our families. These things are critical for survival. In that regard it is a blessing. But when we want to "be right" about an idea or thought that does not comport with reality, this is when our ego's fears are a curse.

The question we should always ask ourselves is how do we know the difference between our illusions and reality? Our egos, whose job is to protect us, do not know the difference between a threat presented by a tiger in the kitchen, and someone raising his voice in anger. So, how are we sure to know the difference? As when selecting a doctor, feedback from objective sources and reflection is the key.

This need to "be right" about what we think and believe is the major block to collaboration toward possibility, which is key to building commitment. If we say people are wrong every time they comes up with an idea, they will stop contributing. Bill McGinnis is a master at listening and collaborating. He puts aside what he believes so he can really listen to his team. This is crucial to building anything.

Feedback-Rich Environment

Early in my career I joined a consulting firm that had coaching and feedback as a primary value. After every meeting I attended, my mentor would ask me, "How were you most effective, and how could you have been even more so?" I would respond as best I could, and if I missed anything he would add his observations. His purpose was twofold: He wanted to be sure that I understood where I needed to grow, and he wanted me to develop the habit of self-reflection.

As time went on, I began to recognize where I was being less effective, and I began to self-correct. If I did not do so, my mentor would remind me. At first this was brutal, but because I knew that this career was my destiny, I continued. I experienced many evenings of frustration with my coaches and myself. But in time, I grew so much that I was offered a partnership. In fact I became known as "the feedback junkie." Management warned people that if they went on a sales call with me, I would be asking them for feedback and coaching both before and after the meeting. My personal and professional growth skyrocketed.

Why Do Great Golfers Need a Coach?

At one time Tiger Woods was the best golfer in the world, but even then he could not see his own swing. He needs coaches because he wants to remain a champion, even after a knee operation. He is a natural athlete, but has had coaching and mentoring since he was five. No champion reaches the top, even with a natural gift, without coaching and mentoring. If you don't have coaches and mentors, you will never unleash your true genius.

This need seems obvious if you observe sports or the arts. No championship teams reach the top without lots of coaching. Yet how many of us have coaches committed to our success? My guess is very few. I started out in life as the child of an immigrant, and was attacked by my peers for being different, displaying learning disabilities, and needing a coach just to get through elementary school. Today I am an author as well as a coach to Fortune 500 CEOs and leaders in all walks of life. Every step of the way I had a coach, sometimes several of them, who cared enough about me to confront my ego and unleash my genius from the bonds of "needing to be right." I can remember when Larry Senn, the founder and CEO of the leadership consulting firm where I wanted to be a partner, talked about me to the whole team:

> *"When Paul came to us he was a diamond in the very rough. He needed a lot of work. But because he is always open to coaching and feedback, I know that there is nothing I cannot teach him."*

Even with this praise, my ego was saying that I was not so bad that I "needed a lot of work," and I nearly got defensive in the face of a great compliment. Our egos want to protect us, even if we could be much better at what we do. I still seek coaching and mentoring because, like Tiger Woods, I want to stay on top of my game.

Being "Right" Blocks Possibility

Ask yourself how many times you have found that your need to "be right" overwhelmed your reasoning and good sense. If you are human, it has been often. As I noted earlier in this chapter, "being right" over the centuries has been important to human survival. It keeps us safe both physically and psychologically, but in other ways it limits our growth.

They don't pay Tiger Woods to "be right." They pay him to win. Sometimes, even with a coach, we would rather be right than win. The feeling of fear from our ego's natural defense mechanism scars us, and we settle for the status quo. In a world where everything is expanding, new records are being set every day, and the economic rules are changing, remaining the same is going backwards. Bob Dylan said, "He who is not busy being born is busy dying." If Tiger Woods settles for being not as good because of injuries, he will fade as other golfers pass him. But I am sure he will not settle.

Everyone, even the greatest saints, have an ego. So, the question you have to ask yourself in each moment is, "Is my ego riding me, or am I riding my ego?" Most often, because there are few champions in the world, the fears from your ego will be riding you.

Despite my use of many coaches and mentors, I still find it hard to admit that I am wrong, even when results seem to indicate that fact. Transcending my ego's fears has not been easy because of my need to "be right." But fortunately, with support from my peers, I can get over my hurts and improve my skills. Fortunately, I've learned the difference between my ego's insecurities and present reality. It can be summed up like this:

"Everyone is my teacher, but only I can liberate myself."

This was a very hard lesson, and I remind myself everyday of this truth. Take this book, for example. I have to give many thanks to my editors, for without their coaching and feedback, it would have been much less effective. If you are not in a feedback-rich environment, resist feedback, or are not able to find a way to liberate yourself from your habits, fears, beliefs, and assumptions, then change yourself or your environment.

All successful people have beliefs, principals, and assumptions that run their lives. The most successful are always learning. In an interview with Piers Morgan on CNN, Tony Bennett, one of the great singers of all time, said at the age of eighty-five, "I am always learning."

If you want to achieve the dreams that are whispering to you from behind your fears, surround yourself with people who have the courage to coach you and always reach beyond. You can't do it alone; no one does.

PRACTICES and ACTIONS

Are you in a feedback-rich environment? If not, it will be much harder to grow your individual or team effectiveness due the effect of your ego. The key to creating this kind of environment is to be open to feedback and coaching, and to practice asking for honest feedback. It is almost as hard giving feedback as it is asking for it, so help your coaches and mentors by doing the following:

1. Be open to the possibility of a better way.

2. Ask for feedback in a way that makes people feel safe.

3. Ask yourself and your team if fear is blocking the way forward.

4. Always say thank you to reward people for their courage.

Powerful commitment starts with possibility. Without seeing possibility individually, as a team or corporation, you will not be able to invent your future, but will remain largely as you are today. As Susan Jeffers says in her book, *Feel The Fear and Do It Anyway*.

So, don't settle for watching others run past you as they invent their futures. Become a feedback junkie.

Chapter 10:

Tap into Imagination and Intention

All of the creations around us were first pictured in someone's imagination. Great works of art, architecture, literature, and engineering all started with a particular vision of an individual or a group of people. If we look into our own lives, we can see things we imagined come true, if only in small ways. That awareness nourishes our intention, which leads to success.

"The first question I ask anyone wanting to get involved with Youth Mentoring Connection is, 'What's your vision for your life?' It thrills most people, even though they do not know how to answer. So immediately we take what we do with our kids and practice it with our employees, our staff, and our board members."

—Tony LoRe, CEO, Youth Mentoring Connection

"Imagination is more important than knowledge."

—Albert Einstein

"I truly believe our thoughts are very powerful. They are so powerful that they can change what ultimately can become our destiny."

—Linda LoRe, CEO, Frederick's of Hollywood

Photo: Sarah Clarehart

Ever since I first read some of the great writers of my day, I imagined I would be a poet and philosopher. As I have matured, I have realized that this was not my imagination; it was my calling doing the imagining, as though an angel kept whispering to me in my dreams, both sleeping and awake.

Consider Henry David Thoreau, Dylan Thomas, Bob Dylan, Camus, Jean Paul Sartre, Winston Churchill, and even Robin Hood, Zorro, and Tarzan. Whether actual humans or fictional characters, these are all people who could see a better future and took action. For me, it has taken years to fully answer this call, and now you are part of it as you read these words.

My most successful work has been about making a difference in people's lives. When I was invited to interview at Senn Delaney Leadership, the vision "Making a difference in the lives of people and the performance of organizations" instantly captured my imagination. It was clearly in sync with my calling.

I have found that when my intention is in line with my calling, images follow. This happens to all of us, but often we resist, thinking we are not good enough, or we just look the other way. As my grandfather told me, "Luck is when preparation meets with opportunity." If you are prepared, you can pounce on opportunities as they occur.

Imagination paints the mental picture of our calling, and prepares us to act when opportunity appears. Without this imagination, we might just miss many opportunities.

Who Wants Yesterday's Frameworks?

Even though Albert Einstein said, "Imagination is more important than knowledge," we often replace our imagination with what are called "best practices," or even worse, habitual old behaviors. While a best practice or behavior worked at one time in your life or business, it will not continue to be a best practice in the face of our constantly changing realities. Here is a story that illustrates this truth in a corporation.

I had been called to Disney to talk with one of their executives about helping him with some organizational development programs. It seemed like a great opportunity. The lobby of their Burbank facility, with pictures of cartoon characters on the walls, was perfect. Creating "The Happiest Place on Earth" was Walt Disney's dream, but at this time, it seemed the place was not as happy as he had envisioned.

Perhaps I could help, or at least that is what one of the coaching brokers in Los Angeles thought. I waited in the lobby for the "meet and greet." The person who recommended me and I were welcomed and sent upstairs to talk with one of their executives. We sat down at a round table in his office and introductions were made.

The questioning to determine if my services fit into their profile began with, "Which instruments do you use to set a baseline?" I explained that I have been coaching and consulting with senior executives for twenty-five years, and so I prefer using my knowledge of human nature. The coaching broker kicked me under the table, and then I added that I am familiar with most instruments. Clearly I had gone off script.

Then the fatal moment occurred. I noticed a copy of Jack Welch's first book, *Winning*, in the center of the table. I was hoping it was an accidental placement, but it turned out to be much more than that.

I thought to myself about the many companies that had adopted someone else's framework, and how I would have to work to bring that organization back to life. Hmmm ... this could be a great consulting opportunity, I thought. But surely Disney was not adopting Jack Welch's framework. I decided to bring the book into the conversation so I said, "I notice Jack Welch's book."

He reached over and put his hand on the book and asked, "Have you read this book?" "Yes," I replied. He explained that it was their Bible.

I have been trained in sales techniques and knew then and there that I should not begin to explain that a framework that works for one company could not work for another. I said to myself, "Wait ..." but my mind rolled on: Frameworks for a company are like thoughts, beliefs, ideas, and other cognitive forms that are only an approximation of reality—not reality itself. We have experiences that cause insight into reality, and then we form cognitive frameworks to describe and categorize those experiences. There is no way that a description of an experience can duplicate the full reality. Unfortunately, many executives navigate the business world as though the thoughts and beliefs recorded in their memory banks are all real. Some are, but many come from a time and context that have passed. This kind of false understanding leads to loss of market share, incorrect business strategies, and the loss of billions of dollars.

I knew I should not say that, but what about explaining that thought precedes manifestation and is, therefore, a key tool for a business-person? After all, imagination is the greatest gift to mankind, but has also proven dangerous. It is clear that human thought is one of the sources of creation. Some say that thought has the power to create reality. There is plenty of evidence to support this view. Architecture, businesses such as General Electric, art, and civilizations are all created by thought.

But, just as thoughts create beautiful realities, they can also create horrible distortions. For example, an anorexic person will look in the mirror and see fat, even though there is none. Such people might be starving them-selves to death, but their thoughts tell them they need to lose weight to be accepted. This is called a cognitive distortion. Of course, this is an extreme example, but all of us experience some kind of distortion. Old business frameworks are cognitive distortions. They do not describe the reality, yet many companies blindly follow them.

Jack Welch's frameworks solved the efficiency problems he was trying to overcome at General Electric. They worked brilliantly because Jack had unleashed his genius and the wisdom of his team to create them. However, the genius that Jack Welch unleashed in the moment to solve complex problems at GE could not possibly work at Disney. So, I said to myself, "No, don't say that yet!"

Then finally I decided to use questions, but I was leading the witness. I said, "What was the key driver of GE's manufacturing companies?" He replied, "Efficiency and productivity." Then I asked, "What is the key driver of success at Disney?" He replied correctly again, "Creativity." Now I thought I had won a great victory, but I had forgotten the key principle I had drummed into my consultant's heads years ago. "Don't ask questions to which you already know the answers. Instead, ask questions that lead to mutual discovery."

Then it happened. I said, "How can a framework developed for a manufacturing company possibly work for a creative company?" I got this glassy stare and some polite conversation, but no real answer. They found another consultant. But later I consoled myself on being right as I watched Disney lose creative allies, as well as its chairman and CEO.

As I gave that advice, I remembered what one of my mentors had asked me years ago: "Do you want to be right, or win?" My answer sounded like Jack Welch: "I want both."

Will Yesterday's Frameworks Work Today?

Scientists have discovered what ancient mystics often have said: the universe, of which we are all part, is a relational grid of energy forms that are continuously emerging and changing. It is like being part of a multidimensional river whose currents affect one another and have no real boundaries. No part of that river is ever the same from moment to moment. The Buddha said, "You cannot step into the same river twice." There is a nature to its flow, but it is never the same. So, we can create a framework that describes the nature of this flow, to build irrigation systems and hydroelectric plants, but there are always unintended consequences. The frameworks have to be adjusted and changed as our understanding of the deeper flows of energy change.

Frameworks Have a Limited Life

A framework is an approximation of the nature of a flow. Consequently, its value is limited by the ever-changing nature of the flow it is describing. The same is true in everyday life. For example, my mind has a framework for how to play basketball successfully that I developed in my youth, but as my body has aged, that framework does not work anymore. Likewise, in every endeavor, from financial markets to managing the environment, we have to adjust our frameworks as the flows change.

Do we wait for our frameworks to fall apart before we change them? The answer seems to be yes. Over history we have become attached to yesterday's frameworks, even as the civilizations formed by those frameworks fell all around us. Why does it continue to be difficult to adapt to the changes in the flow of our world? This raises a big question—in fact, the most important question for each of us: Are we adjusting our frameworks to comport with the reality of the moment? If not, our success will surely be limited.

Examine your beliefs and assumptions, and question all of them. You may want to keep some of them for a while, but you will find that most need upgrading or eliminating so you can invent your future.

Commitment and Intention

What is the difference between an idle thought and an intention powerful enough to invent the future? Some say if you want something to be so, think about or write down your desires and it will come true. Others point out that intention has to be a strongly held belief. Goethe said, "The moment one definitely commits oneself, then Providence moves too. All sorts of things occur to help one that would never otherwise have occurred." It seems to me that intention is more like a feeling than a thought—like working your way into a wave when you are surfing. As a friend of mine who is a Harvard PhD and surfer said, "You cannot think your way into a wave, you have to feel it."

Connect to Who You Really Are

Like the surfer connected to a force of nature that propels him forward, our intentions have more power when they are flowing with the natural current of our lives. We all have a natural current and rhythm within us that is part of the greater flow. It's what makes us unique, or who we really are. When we resist this current, which some call purpose, we suffer. When we know it deeply, and learn to swim with it, we move forward with grace and ease in an almost magical manner.

"Know Thyself"—It's a Feeling or a Knowing

Knowing how to connect with the larger current that you are part of on a deep level is genius. The secret is to feel the difference between emotions that come from your thoughts and beliefs, and the feeling of being connected to your unique river. Once you know this, you can begin to expand yourself while moving forward in your natural current. You can use that intention to create new realities that change the flow of your life. You then can move with grace and ease to create something that is a natural extension of your deepest purpose while adding to the beauty of the world around you.

As Matt Witte, managing partner of Marwit Investment Management LLC, said, "Intention works to create the future when you are connected to your purpose." Examine your calling, as I have suggested, and become committed to your life's purpose.

PRACTICES and ACTIONS

Our calling or purpose builds commitment. Our purpose often comes from early childhood experiences. Research done by Dan Buettner in his book *Blue Zones: Lessons for Living Longer From the People Who've*

Lived the Longest indicates that purpose is key to health and living longer, as well as performance.

> *"Purpose can come from a job or a hobby, especially if you can immerse yourself completely in it. Claremont University psychologist Dr. Mihály Csíkszentmihályi best describes this feeling in his book,* Flow: The Psychology of Optimal Experience. *He defines flow as a Zen-like state of total oneness with the activity at hand in which you feel fully immersed in what you're doing."* —**Dan Buettner.** *The Blue Zones, Second Edition*

Find these times in your life.

1. Go through your early life and relive all of those times when you were totally committed to something. Analyze each for the steps that worked for you and make the practice of repeating those steps to face future challenges.

2. Imagine how the essence of your greatest experiences can help you build your level of commitment to something that is important to you.

3. Look back again in your life for a theme. Who were your heroes and what did they stand for? Why did you love them? I can see myself as a boy, swinging from a tree, pretending to be Robin Hood or Tarzan. What did you love, before the demands of the world made you put down those dreams? Go to your journal and write down these imaginings, as they are surely messages from your angels.

4. What are the deep cords that resonate with your heart, which never lies? Write these down in your journal.

5. Remember all the times you failed to reach your goals? Ask yourself the question Lloyd Wallis always asks: "On a scale of one to ten, how committed are you?"

6. Notice how your need to "be right" about an old framework or belief about your life interfered with your success.

7. See which of those beliefs or frameworks are still operating in your life. Then begin the process of letting them go, and focus your attention on your calling and how to integrate that into your life's work.

None of this is easy, but as a successful friend of mine once said, "I did not sign up for easy."

PART FIVE:

RESPOND
TO REALITY

Photo: Sarah Clarehart

Chapter 11

Respond to Present Reality

Every moment you spend away from the present moment is like the difference between enjoying delicious food and eating a picture of food on a menu. The menu is harder to chew, sticks inside your guts, and is tasteless, much like having your concerns about the past or future dominate your consciousness. They tend to be useless and unpleasant. Conversely, being in the moment is like biting into a fresh piece of fruit—full of life, delicious, and easily digested. Every moment you spend away from the present is robbing you of life itself.

11: Respond to Present Reality

"In October 2008, we saw a material and sustained shift in the spending patterns of our advertising customers. We had to adapt quickly. We laid off people—never an easy thing to do—and focused on rapidly retooling the business. As we now know, in the fourth quarter of 2008, the great recession began … but we were ready. We started hiring again in December, and had a record 2009 and 2010. A competitor three times our size that wasn't able to make the shift went out of business."

—Heath Clarke, former CEO, Local Corporation

Photo: Sarah Clarehart

Are You Here Now or Somewhere Else?

After reading my first book, a friend of mine who passed away some time ago was inspired to tell me the following story. Luis Villalobos was founder of the Tech Coast Angels, and a very successful business person. He told me about a day driving his beloved Porsche. A car in front of him had stopped suddenly. Lewis said that he went into "the zone" right away, and everything moved in super slow motion. Being "in the zone" is when you are completely into your authentic self, and into the work you are doing.

In this instance, Luis slammed on his breaks, swerving into the next lane to avoid the collision. After looking back on what he had done, it seemed impossible, yet while he was in the zone it had seemed simple. His ability to be highly present had saved his life and the lives of others. This ability did not come without the practice of being present in boardrooms, and in dealing with difficult negotiations. He learned to respond to present reality, not to simply react from habit.

We are all creatures of habit. When we have had either successful or unsuccessful events in our life, we form a habitual way of reacting, which may or may not be appropriate to the moment. As the flow of cause and effect moves forward, habitual strategies, good or bad, lose their effectiveness. Additionally, it takes us time to select among the various habitual reactions. As we are considering what to do the flow of cause and effect moves past us. We are too late and often wrong.

This is why professional athletes practice being "in the zone," as well as developing their physical skills. Championship teams spend more time "in the zone" than those who do not have a winning record, all else being equal. Luis understood this and often talked about how important it is for leaders.

As in the case of many of our journeys, shit happens! If we are not practiced at being in the present, these sudden events can destroy us and the futures we intend to build. We often go forward in the manner we had intended, regardless of someone stopping in front of us. We are thinking about something that had happened, or something that might happen, instead of being present, which can be fatal to our plans.

By the way, Luis did not die in a car accident. He died of natural causes.

> *"The companies that are succeeding right now have leaders who have a personal practice of mind-stilling and centeredness, using exercise, meditation, or yoga. These practices are quite helpful. They help leaders come into the workplace and exude a certain calm, peace, centeredness, balance, and confidence. I learned a lot of these from athleticism, in sports such as surfing, cycling, and fly fishing. When you get into a zone, a tremendous power and confidence fills your being."* —**Casey Sheahan, President and CEO, Patagonia**

Is the Present Moment the Only Portal to the Future?

When I lived in New York City, a famous Soviet ballerina defected. Her first performance as a free woman was in the Winter Garden Theatre. It was Swan Lake. At her moment to shine, a blanket of white light filled the stage and suddenly she leaped from the platform into freedom. The audience gasped in wonderment. There was a moment of stillness full of beauty and tears. She went on to dance like a goddess, flowing heart and soul to the music. Like Luis, she was "in the zone." She was totally present and fully expressing her heart's desires.

What is the difference between presence and not being present? Our thoughts are constructed of our memories from the past. In dealing with different situations we form beliefs and patterns of thinking. We use these like a roadmap to understand challenges and experiences we face in the present. Something happens and we check in to our beliefs and assumptions, and then react as before. Thoughts and beliefs are most valuable for planning, but in a moment of truth they are too slow. While they are useful, they pale in power and effectiveness to responding to the flow of cause and effect like a dancer in the zone, leaping across the stage at a historic moment.

You might ask, "If you are flowing with the moment, how do you create the future?" Here is what I have found: Imagine the world is a dance floor and the rhythm and flow of the band represents the "life force," which drives the flow of creation.

The dance hall is rocking. The band seems irresistible to some, yet others stand against the wall not knowing how to jump in, and many are not even aware of the dance. They have heard people talk about it, but can't seem to hear or feel the flow of the music. Those who feel it deeply dance like gods and goddesses in the middle of the floor, creating a vortex of energy and motion that draws new dancers into their circle.

The band, the life force, naturally lures people onto the floor to dance in a rhythm and harmony that seems to come from outside of them. Of those on the dance floor, many dance out of rhythm most of the time, but have moments of grace. Others have a routine that works for them, but only captures a small part of the rhythm.

Some have a routine, but experiment momentarily with new movements, and then go back to what they know. Those who feel the music deeply add rhythms and counter-rhythms, and seem to be an extension of the life force that passes through the band. Without knowing, many start to follow the waves of energy coming from the leaders, and the overall quality of the dance improves.

At some point, magic occurs. The beauty and energy of the lead dancers is so compelling that the band itself is drawn into the dance, creating new rhythms and flows to challenge those on the floor. The band and the dancers join to create new realities. The life force creates life, and life influences the life force. It's symbiotic, just as the band creates the rhythm, flow, and changes, incorporating the lead dancers' energy.

The only way to create the future is to engage, like the dancers, with the rhythm and flow of the present. By doing so, you become a co-creator, dancing to the heartbeat of life. It is not about wishing and hoping as the popular book, *The Secret*, would suggest. The various rhythms and flows of your life and business markets are subsets of the life force that animates everything. Both can be influenced in the manner just described. Great leaders have discovered and mastered this secret.

The flow of our lives, business needs, and even a basketball game, are like the complex themes, harmonies, and rhythms in music. So are the winds and currents that circle around our planet. There is no substitute for practice, so it is important to spend lots of time dancing with the rhythm and flow of the moment.

When I dance with the rhythm and flow, life is profound, beautiful, and creative. I can feel the future emerging in the moment with my heart. I have learned this through practice.

My heart is my inner compass. It lets me know the difference between my thoughts about the flow of cause and effect, and the actual flow. We all have to practice recognizing the difference between the emotions that come from our wounds, and those precious feelings that come from our genius.

Knowing how to access your natural wisdom will activate your inner compass—your true compass. Having this compass helps you walk with the wind of the life force at your back and in your heart. As you understand that thoughts and beliefs can provide a roadmap, but are not accurate descriptions of the full reality of the territory, you will learn when to let go of thoughts and beliefs and simply be present.

The only way to be present is to empty your mind of old thoughts and beliefs. If you do that, your understanding of the reality of the moment will be unfiltered. In all matters of mastery, the final step is letting go of your thoughts and dancing with the flow of cause and effect.

Consciousness

Enlightenment is the experience of unfiltered reality. Even a single moment of this kind of experience can change our lives. But enlightenment is only the beginning. After enlightenment comes expanding consciousness. This journey is infinite. As we expand our consciousness, the experience affects our thinking, and we are enriched.

Peter Russell, a renowned physicist, author, and meditation teacher, has some intriguing perspectives on consciousness. Take a look. 🔗

The more expanded our consciousness, the clearer the path ahead. We act upon the emergence of needs and wants in our marketplace, our teams, our communities, and our world. We see opportunities in the very earliest stages of emergence, and act on that emergence for the greater good.

Presence Leads to Performance

Larry Senn, founder of Senn Delaney Leadership, had been a gymnast, and later coach of the gymnastics team for UCLA, and when I asked him what he learned about performance from that experience, he said,

> *"It was only when I no longer knew the judges were there, when I no longer knew the crowd was there, when I just connected with my art, my performance, that I could truly perform. For me it was floor exercise. I would be nervous. I would look at the judge, and he would nod his head, and somehow I had to just immerse myself in what I was going to do. When I became conscious of how I was doing, I did not do as well. I think life is like that."*

Larry realized that if he thought about what he was doing, it would take him away from the present moment and destroy his performance. Thoughts interrupt our presence because they are only approximations of reality that we become attached to, and an approximation of reality will not keep us "in the zone" or any other state of mind that generates extraordinary performance. We must learn to clear thoughts from our consciousness when we are taking action.

Acknowledge Present Reality

In a business situation, even when you are looking for the right answer, if you are not aware of the present reality, you are going to be in big trouble. We just do not like our thoughts to be wrong. However, the flow of cause and effect moves forward, with or without our active involvement. In business, we don't like to be aware of the present reality, particularly if it contradicts something we believe. We tend to distort reality to fit our preconceived thoughts about it.

Tim Pulido, president and CEO of Campero USA and Pollo Campero International, a seasoned restaurant leader, told me this story that took place when he was CEO of Shakey's Pizza:

> "The previous year we had launched a product that was inconsistent with what we stood for as a brand. It was called Big Foot. It was basically a big, cheap, low-cost pizza. We were following the competition, which was doing similar things. When it was launched people were really ticked off. They said things like, 'Wait a minute, this is not pizza!'

> "Yet, since abandoning Big Foot was not the executive team's idea, I had a hard time convincing them, even in the face of a consumer revolt, that we needed to change direction. I had to get the team to recognize that we had made a strategic error. No one wanted to admit that this was not consistent with our brand. So we went back to the consumer—and this is also a critical principle of creating a compelling story or a compelling picture."

After abandoning Big Foot, the result of their consumer research, among other things, produced the cheese-stuffed crust, which became very popular. Their compelling picture was, "So good that you want to eat the crust first." Again questioning existing assumptions and habits, while looking to the future to invent something new, is almost always the right answer given the rapid change in most industries. It is not easy, because people get attached to their old ideas and habits.

Leaders such as Tim know they always have to have a clear line of sight to present reality versus what we assume to be true. If you are starting a business, be sure your picture of success is not created in a subjective vacuum, but is a result of your knowledge of your customers, even if they include your boss or brand within your company. Always acknowledge reality by practicing presence no matter how it makes you feel. Our egos hate to be wrong, but ask yourself, do you want to be right, or do you want to win?

Acknowledging Reality Is Difficult

I'll say it again: There is no true reality outside of the present moment! Thought, though very useful for planning, is at best an approximation of reality, not reality itself. Knowing this at your very deepest level will enable you to let go of your thoughts and respond to the flow of the present.

Our egos always want to be right. So we distort reality to fit into our beliefs and assumptions, while the actual flow of cause and effect carries on right past us. A baseball player who does not keep his eye and consciousness on the ball will miss the opportunity for a home run. Likewise, each moment is an opportunity for an insight, or a deep connection with a friend or stranger. Each moment presents opportunities to dance with the rhythm and flow of our lives. Each moment offers both wonderment and lessons.

As I mention in Chapter 1, my chiropractor, Dr. Wolff, was shown a picture of a man in a magazine by his staff, who told him, "He looks just like you." The staff made funny faces when he said, "He does not look at all like me." Dr. Wolff argued, but then went into the bathroom and held the magazine up beside his reflection in the mirror. He realized that the picture of himself he held in his mind no longer looked like him. He had lost his hair and had aged. Somehow he just did not realize this until that moment. He told me that this had caused him several days of sadness, of being out of balance.

We can all relate to this. I know when I walk by the basketball court where I used to play with my sons years ago, I feel like I could just jump in and play again. Once I watched some guys play, and thought to myself, I could beat them! I had my basketball shoes on, so I joined in, and as you might imagine, I did not win or even compete. I stopped when my hips and knees became painful, realizing that I could seriously hurt myself. The pain continued for over a week. My mind was stronger than my body, and totally out of sync with the reality of my age and condition. This illustrates the danger of not acknowledging reality.

To begin any journey, or plan a successful venture, you must know the reality of where you are now. Living in self-deceit, while it may feel good, will not feed success and happiness. Eventually, present reality will knock you down. This is why a rigorous examination of present reality is the hallmark of success.

Living under illusions will eventually result in disillusionment and serious mistakes. No matter how committed a team is to a mission, having the wrong starting point can make your plans useless. Knowing the "good, the bad, and the ugly" about any situation you are facing empowers you to build plans that are targeted and effective.

The challenge here is that people hate to be wrong, and they find ways to make reality match their beliefs. This is the problem with the belief in "positive thinking." It often skips acknowledging reality and moves too quickly to planning and action.

Pessimists, because of their negative beliefs about life, give up at this step, feeling overwhelmed and hopeless. A plan that is not grounded in reality, no matter how clear and committed its supporters may be, will lead you over a cliff. Presence is always the key.

If someone were to give you directions to Chicago, and thought that you were in Los Angeles, when in fact you were in Miami, you would become lost no matter how precise the guidance. A leader and his or her team must honestly face weaknesses and misconceptions to invent the future. It is best to always come back to this imperative.

Worry Is Thought on Steroids

If Larry Senn had been worrying about his scores before he began his gymnastics routine, he would not have succeeded. Studies show that most things we worry about never happen. Is this because the worry prevents bad things from happening, or is it just a waste of energy? My first wife always said to me, "I have to worry for both of us." If worry was an indicator of future events, it would be more predictive than it actually appears to be. Certainly, people who worry a lot do not seem happy and often suffer from stress. But, are they all saving us from tragedies with their collective worries?

Worry is a pattern of circular thoughts focused on a particular event or possibility that makes us anxious. We believe that something bad might happen in the future, such as losing our jobs, and we think about that possibility over and over again. These circular thoughts fill our consciousness and we feel more and more stressed. Our state of mind deteriorates and in some cases nervous breakdowns occur. What happens is our consciousness narrows to focus on a worry and filters out everything else, including pleasant sensations that come naturally with day-to-day living, such as enjoying a beautiful morning.

Additionally, because we seem to have a need to be right about our thinking, we actually begin to select things that prove our worries to be justified. We become taken up by a worry death spiral.

What Are You Missing Because of Worry?

Because our consciousness narrows and becomes invested in being right about our worries, we miss most everything else. We often fail to connect with the people in our lives who are most important to us. A beautiful day seems dark. As the pattern of worry sets in, even wonderful events in our lives bring on the feeling of impending doom, with thoughts like "this can't last," "this is the quiet before the storm," or "I don't deserve this." We also are so focused on our worries that we overlook obvious solutions to our problems. We go to work in a bad mood, and people wonder what is wrong with us. Someone, maybe our boss, might start to become concerned about our attitude, which may lead to a layoff. Then our mind will say to us, "See, I was right to worry; I just did not worry hard enough."

How Can You Stop Worrying?

The first step in letting go of worry is realizing that thought at best is only an approximation of reality, and at worst can drive you crazy. Yes I am saying this again; it is important to understanding life. As a poet, I often try to inspire people by describing the deep beauty of the world we live in, but even with my skill with words it is still just an approximation of the beauty I experience.

There seems to be a deep intelligence within the formless, which expresses itself in form. You can call it the flow of heaven, the life force, the grace of God, divine intention, the great intelligence, the great spirit, or natural intelligence.

This intelligence is continuously expressing itself in form. Everything we see around us has arisen from it: the trees, flowers, oceans, fishes and, yes, each of us as human beings. We are an expression of divine intention, or as many say, God. This "Great Intelligence" is woven into every fiber of our being and drives life itself. It is always there within you and all around you. If you are consciously aware of this reality, your entire being shines from within and your thoughts are filled with joy and wonder.

Collaborating with this intelligence, which literally pulsates within you, creates thoughts and actions that we call an expression of genius.

I can tell you that, after years of practice as a writer, although these thoughts may inspire you, it is only an approximation of what I experience. Realizing that thoughts are only an approximation of reality will change the way we deal with them. If thoughts such as these inspire you to higher levels of consciousness and happiness, then they are useful, yet only an approximation. If, like worry, they narrow your consciousness and create stress, then they are useless, if not harmful.

Just as you naturally pull your hand from a flame when you feel the heat, learn to let go of thoughts that create psychological pain. As you move your consciousness away from your thoughts, you will become filled with natural beauty and grace. It is nature's, or God's, way of directing you ... and yes, it is that simple! "Don't worry, be happy."

Like the gymnast who achieves a perfect ten, there is no worry or thought involved in the moment of truth. When standing before the judges, worry could ruin years of practice and preparation. If you form the habit of presence, whatever you do will be much more effective.

Perceiving and Responding to Reality

Thought is a mechanism to describe reality, not a method to perceive the complex flow of cause and effect. A basketball player "in the zone" responds to the flow of the game, and changes that flow by his or her response. Later, with insight from being in the zone, the team might use thought to adjust the game plan. But only the momentary actions of the players in rhythm and flow of the game will influence the outcome. The same is true in business and our lives, which are a much more complex team endeavor.

Wisdom of the Moment

All of the great leaders I have worked with know how to achieve the state of Integrative Presence, or being "in the zone," even though they may not understand the nature of this state of mind. They have experienced being connected to something that supercharges their own knowledge. They speak reverently about this connection in private, but rarely talk about it to the press. It just seems too outside the norm for stockholders and the public. But knowing and connecting to the wisdom of the moment is essential for leaders in business or individuals trying to invent their futures. Markets move quickly, often with little warning, and the wise leader can feel the moving currents. At each moment, like a surfer, the conscious leaders are so present they take advantage of trends as they emerge. The same is can be true for all of us.

PRACTICES and ACTIONS

I remind myself often that everyone is my teacher, but only I can free myself. If I were to have a tattoo, it would say those words.

1. Remind yourself daily that everyone is your teacher, but that only you can free yourself. I recommend you practice this for a week, and write what you notice in your journal. Notice how people respond to you. Notice the nature of your feelings, both good and bad.

2. Notice how people react to you in all your interactions; for example, with waiters, clerks and friends. In this manner the world around you becomes your mirror.

3. As the week progresses you will become more present and will start adjusting how you dance with the rhythm and flow of your life. Notice this too, and write about it in your journal.

4. Meditating is simply practicing being in the moment. Find a simple practice that works for you. Any practice that brings you to the present will give you a visceral experience of the difference between eating real food and eating pictures of food on the menu.

5. Remember, there is no substitute for practice.

Chapter 12:

Cultivate Intention and Purpose

What is it like to be around committed people? They seem to be surrounded by a great intensity, an attraction that draws you into whatever they are doing. They appear to shine. No matter how badly things go, they get up and try even harder the next time. They may lose a battle, but they will not lose the war. Sometimes they just drive you crazy, but most times you admire them, even if you don't agree with their point of view. Does their energy travel over some network causing all sorts of things to occur? Yes it does.

"When something resonates to our purpose in life, when something resonates to a contribution that we want to make, when something resonates to a service that we want to perform, there is a solidity and a recognition that takes place within you. When you follow this resonance, this inner guidance, this experience, it becomes easier for you to recognize over time.

"When this resonance is present, it does not matter whether it involves a product, a technology, or a service. The emergence of your purpose, your inner calling, will begin coloring your life with a mystical quality and a depth of meaning that far exceeds the goal of making a profit."

—Lawerence Koh, President, International Diversified Products

"I believe that intention works to create the future when you are connected to your purpose, or who you are meant to be."

—Matt Witte, Managing Partner, Marwit Investment Capital, LLC

A connection pulsates between purpose and intention. Without that connection to your purpose, or natural genius, intention becomes just a wish that we struggle to create. There is no flow, no natural grace. Larry Senn, said to me:

> "I am at my highest when I am talking about the work I do with people. When I am doing that, I am in a flow state. It is when I am connected to my purpose that I am at my best. I have access to an intelligence beyond myself. It is so startling that at times I say, 'where did that come from?'"

Much has been written about the power of intention or purpose. Goethe, a well-known German thinker, said:

> "Until one is committed, there is hesitancy, the chance to draw back, always ineffectiveness concerning all acts of initiative and creation. There is one elementary truth, the ignorance of which kills countless ideas and splendid plans: that the moment one definitely commits oneself, then providence moves too, all sorts of things occur to help one that would never otherwise have occurred. A whole stream of events issues from the decision raising in one's favor all manner of unforeseen events, meetings and material assistance, which no man could have dreamed would have come his way. Whatever you can do or dream you can, begin it. Boldness has genius, power and magic in it. Begin it now!"

We have all experienced this idea in some way or another. Look back into your own life and see how true this is. I can count a number of occasions when I was totally committed to something and, in fact, as Goethe said, "All sorts of things occurred to help."

As science has proven, all things are connected by a force that is beyond time and space. Our intention seems to travel over this natural network.

Even more powerful is a committed team. Have you ever had to face a truly committed team in sports or business? It is very intimidating. They have this look in their eyes and humble confidence in their voice. I like to watch sports interviews prior to playoff games. Sometimes you can tell which team is truly committed to winning, and which one is only saying, "We are going to do our best." The team that wins is always the one that intends to win, but not with just words. Instead, they have a certain energy. No matter what happens on the road of their intent, they find ways to reach the goal. That is what drives successful people. In my experience as a CEO coach and leadership consultant, the same is true for business teams.

Are You Chasing Life, or Letting Life Chase You?

Michael Jordan was a star player for the Chicago Bulls. He won scoring titles and most valuable player recognitions, but his team could not seem to win a National Basketball Association championship. Phil Jackson, his coach, could see that he was chasing the game. He said to Michael, "Let the game come to you." Phil taught him to be centered, which created a vortex that brought the game to him, instead of chasing the game. He was always trying to save the game by his own effort, which is why he scored so many points. When he began to let the game come to him, his team got involved, and instead of him chasing opposing players, they used their energy to chase him. Suddenly the team's game expanded to another level and they won championships.

Are you chasing life and missing or overshooting the rhythm and flow? Are you working hard, and yet the magic is not happening? Do you wonder why others succeed and don't seem to be working as hard?

First ask yourself if you are fully trained in life. Do you understand the game of life, or the endeavor in life you are pursuing?

Second, you have to understand how life works, just as Michael Jordan understood the game of basketball. You may be running past opportunities, having to double back, only to find that those opportunities had already closed. If so, you are chasing life instead of letting life come to you. Stop, and work on becoming centered in yourself until you feel the joy of living in your heart. Master each breath, still your mind and walk as if you are dancing with an invisible lover.

The "life force" is infusing us in every moment, but often we are too busy looking ahead to notice.

Unleash your talent from the chase, and deepen how you live in the present. Then dance with the rhythm and flow as it comes to you.

Teamwork and Intention

As we move toward our picture of the future, we cannot anticipate everything that might happen. We have to respond to the curve balls the world throws at us. For example, in the process of reinventing his company, Bill McGinnis, CEO of National Technical Systems, told me this story:

> *"The clarity we shared allowed flexibility and experimentation as unforeseen challenges arose. We moved like a team 'in the zone' and found a new path to the picture we all could see. Had we not come together, we could have actually taken our company slowly down the wrong path, and the turn-around may not have worked.*

> *"It is important to know that during the process you don't have to be a hundred percent right. When we're not, let's adjust; let's change; let's talk about it; let's figure it out. If we still haven't figured it out, let's start again.*

> *"Working with openness, flexibility, and commitment to each other is the key. I would say that honest discussions with a true level of caring for one another allows you to make the changes needed to invent your future."*

The strength of this commitment gave Bill and his team the courage to adjust until their actions got on target. But because they knew the right outcome, they were able to adjust their actions until they were in the flow.

Who is on your team, and how deeply do they know the right answer, or picture of the future? Most CEOs and other successful people have hundreds of people helping them. If you are trying to go it alone, you will not succeed. No one has ever succeeded without help from friends.

So many leaders that I have worked with want to build a "dream team" of triple-A people. Often these individuals are hard to find, and as soon as they get together their egos clash. While interviewing Henry Walker, CEO of Farmers and Merchants Bank, the highest-rated midsized bank in Southern California, I discovered that he plays polo. He explained his process for purchasing a horse:

> *"Our family plays polo, and, in fact, is the first to field four generations on a team. Now, I am not comparing people to horses, but there are many lessons that come out of sports. When I buy a new horse, it is not always the best horse money can buy, but the best horse for me. I look for a horse whose natural traits match with my own. After all, we are a team."*

As mentioned in the full version of Walker's story in this book's prologue, the same is true for business partners, employees, or other people who might help you manifest your new future. It is more important to find someone whose circumstances in life fit with what you want them to do. Be sure your partner's or employee's contribution fits into to where they are in their life.

Intention Uses Forces Outside of Time and Space

Throughout life we all have a glimpse or two into deeper realities but often forget about these experiences, or think perhaps they were dreams, luck, or hallucinations. We have moments of wonder and insight that pass too quickly. Maybe the muses or angels are providing us with a flash of insight, or perhaps we are tapping into something we do not yet understand. The mysteries of how people with strong intention seem to magically have things occur, seemingly out of their will, have always puzzled humanity. Bell's Theorem implies that all things are connected and in relationship. Later, as empirical proof was developed, it turned out that the force that connects things is, in fact, beyond time and space. It follows that it would not be crazy to think that intention is connected to a force from a dimension most don't understand.

Purpose Feeds Energy

> *"It takes a monumental amount of effort and labor and work to run this organization. People ask me why I don't burn out, and they warn me that I am going to burn out. My answer is always, 'I don't believe I can burn out, if am always in my purpose.' If I stray from my purpose or calling, I don't get the energy. My vision, my reason for being, my passion gives me all the energy I need."* —Tony LoRe, CEO, Youth Mentoring Connection

When you have that purpose, you need targeted actions, which are a little different than goals. Everyone has financial goals or legal goals, but in terms of the people in your company, you need to consider whether they are on target or not. Do they know what to do in every situation, no matter what, without any advice? When a very odd situation comes up, do they know how to hit that target, moment to moment, day to day?

Purpose is one of those words, like *God*, that has multiple connotative and denotative meanings. So let me define what I understand about purpose at this moment.

We are all unique spiritual beings. Each of us is a note in the music of the universe. Each of us is like a tuning fork. Our first step is to understand our note and resonate with our part in the universal symphony, or the flow. That brings joy and happiness beyond description. Then, with practice, our being resonates with other beings. At that point we learn to feel the resonance in others, just as a C tuning fork will resonate with another C tuning fork. Then we can sync our lives with our own natural resonance, which attracts the very flow of cause and effect for which we are most suited.

Once that happens, when opportunities present themselves due to the law of attraction, instead of missing them, we see and ride that flow like a surfer at the perfect point in a wave.

PRACTICES and ACTIONS

Look back in your life to a time when your intention was totally clear. This intention can be good or bad. For example, when I moved from turning around companies in the 70s, I took a self-help course. I was amazed at how the facilitator brought total strangers together almost as a family committed to each other's success. At the end of that seminar, watching the facilitator summarize, I said to myself that this is what I will do the rest of my life. I could see how it would have worked so much better than the methods I used in business. At that moment my intention was so clear that later, as I took all their courses to learn their methodology, people began to confuse me with the actual facilitator.

Later, when I offered a few words during a meeting of Beyond War, a group organized to end global conflict, a woman came up to me and asked if I knew the people at Senn Delaney Leadership. I said no. She said, "You have got to meet them." When I did I found out that they had mastered using this technology in business and were hiring. Against all odds, I was hired, became a partner, and spent twenty-five years doing what I had seen myself do as I watched the facilitator summarize earlier. My intention was clear, and it moved providence. Try to find similar experiences in your life.

1. Write down stories in your journal about a time when you could see yourself doing something, and succeeded. Capture the moment of intention, and then describe how you overcame all obstacles and how providence helped you with unexpected opportunities.

2. Notice how conflicting intentions also stopped you at other times, such as when you wanted something, but felt deep inside you did not deserve it.

3. Capture as many stories, negative and positive, where your true internal intention became reality.

4. Analyze these times in your life and look at what intentions you are holding now. Remember the phrase, "Be careful what you wish for—it might come true."

Chapter 13

Gather the Courage to Act

One of the most persistent fears we face is that of the unknown. We do not like walking into dark rooms, or rooms full of strangers. No matter how well we prepare for the future, no matter how clear or compelling our vision, it is still unknown. There is a point where you just have to gather the courage to step into the unknown. Courage is required to invent your future. Winston Churchill knew that when he said on national radio, after the Nazis defeated his armies, bombed his cities, and blockaded his navy, that all he promised was "blood, sweat, and tears," and that "we will never surrender." His courage saved a nation and our world.

"People don't like change, but change is ultimately progress. It's not how big you are—it's how rapidly you can adapt. We've been very lucky to have developed a real-time business with a team that embraces change.

"Ironically, looking back over five years of business, what worked five years ago for us doesn't work today. So you have to be prepared to continue to innovate and adapt. Basically, if we did not adapt we wouldn't be here today."

—Heath Clarke, former CEO, Local Corporation

"Fear is the most crippling emotion that an organization or a person can have."

—Linda LoRe, CEO, Frederick's of Hollywood

"I can do this better."

—Jim Jannard, CEO and Founder, Oakley and Red Digital Cinema

Photo: Sarah Clarehart

To earn my way through college, I got a job during high school selling Cutco Knives to housewives. When I first started, my sales manager, Steve Gothller, was driving me in his car when I said to him, "Not everybody is gonna buy a full set of knives; not everybody can afford to buy these." Each set was priced at $365; in 1968 that was a lot of money. I had sold smaller sets, but never had the courage to make the big ask.

Steve said to me, "Okay, I'll tell you what I'm gonna do. While we are driving, you point to somebody and I'll sell them the complete set. I mean anyone. I'll show you how fucked-up you are."

We were driving down an alley when I saw a teenager working on a car. I said to Steve, "That is the person I want you to sell a complete set of knifes to."

Steve turned around, got out of the car, approached the young man and asked for directions, which was part of his regular routine to break the ice. Steve said, "Working on your car, huh?"

The young man replied, "Yes, sir."

Steve then asked him, "What do you do? Are you in high school or what?"

The boy said, "Well, sir, I'm going to Vietnam in about three months to serve my country."

Steve said, "I'm proud of you defending the country." Then he paused, looked the kid in the eye and said, "A lot of boys don't come back, you know that."

The kid said, "Yes, sir, I know, I know."

Steve then asked him, "Would you be interested in a gift for your mother? Something that she'll use every day of her life? Something she will always remember you by?"

The young guy exclaimed, "Wow, that would be great!"

Steve nodded his head, put up one finger and said, "Just hang on. I think I have something in the car that is just right." He came back with his case and a big poodle stuffed animal. He handed the poodle to the young man and said, "Here, give this to your mother, as a gift from me. But that is not what I am talking about."

He opened up his case and laid the complete set of knives out on the hood of his car. In that moment I knew I was about to get a lesson in courage. The surgical-steel blades were guaranteed to remain sharp for a lifetime, and had ebonite handles fitted for the natural curves of the hand. They shined in the sun. I will never forget the look on the boy's face.

Steve then went through the entire pitch, and somewhere about halfway through, the boy said, "I will take everything, the complete set." Steve glanced over at me with a grin of a cat that had just swallowed a mouse. The kid paid on the spot and in cash, with money he had been saving to give to his mother before he left for the Vietnam war. Steve hugged him and told him he was a role model for others, and a true hero.

Steve turned to me and motioned for us to walk to the car, saying one last goodbye to the young man. We got in, Steve started the motor, and we pulled away. Just as I thought I would get out of this without a big lecture, he pulled the car around the corner and stopped under a big tree. He turned to me and said, "You need to believe in yourself and this fantastic product. You need to develop the courage to act, the courage to ask for the order. I hope this will help you to find your inner strength. I know you will find it, because I believe in you."

I sold those knives throughout college to earn my way, and my mother had a complete set until the day she died, and they never got dull.

Targeted Action Plans

The problem businesses often face is that when things are not going well, leaders change their mission instead of adjusting the action plans. This means that they did not do the work I have talked about earlier in the book. If you know and are committed to the mission, you will know to change the plan, not the mission or target. With the right plan, a team will surpass competitors while learning about themselves. Even at the final step, there may be obstacles, doubts, and fears to overcome. Be on guard for hesitation. A leader must not falter due to the team's fears. Once discovered you must move relentlessly towards the target, working your way around obstacles that will arise.

Courage to Act

The courage to confront your fears and those of the team sets a true leader apart from someone who knows the answer but lacks the courage to act and lead.

When Jim Jannard, founder and former CEO of Oakley, and founder and current CEO of Red Digital Cinema, looked at sunglasses and digital motion-picture products, he said, "I can do this better." And he did, with both. Currently, more than 70 percent of motion pictures you see in the theater are shot with Red Digital cameras. Oakley, which he founded before Red Digital, is not only a model company, it is the quality brand of sunglasses for sports of all kinds. He certainly has the courage to overcome his fears and act.

Another CEO with courage is Linda LoRe. Faced with many naysayers, she turned around and saved Frederick's of Hollywood.

> *"I never paid attention to the naysayers. I mean, I heard what they were saying, I noticed it, but I didn't let that get in my way, because fear is the most crippling emotion that an organization can have, or a person can have.*

"I truly believe our thoughts are very powerful. They are so powerful that they can change what ultimately can become our destiny.

"What I have been able to do is to separate the naysayers, and say, okay, I'm going to prove them wrong; or, okay, I hear what they are saying, and I will validate. If there is something valid that comes out of them, I will use that for my benefit. Because, generally speaking, naysayers are just afraid."
—Linda LoRe, CEO, Frederick's of Hollywood

Our Own Naysayer

We often become our own naysayer. We become critical of ourselves due to fear, even when we know we are on the right path. I know this is true for myself. Often I will think, "Who will really want to read this book? Who are you to think you have something to say?" It comes up for me every day. I just do what Linda says: I hear myself, recognize the fear, and move forward anyway.

My ability to do this is enhanced by knowing my purpose and intention. If I had not done the work discussed earlier in this book, my "critical parent" probably would have won out.

Linda LoRe was facing bankruptcy and liquidators who were in place before she took over. They made their money by selling assets. She knew this was not right, and that the company and brand had value, as well as 1,800 employed workers and vendors who made a living from the enterprise.

Linda knew the answer was not liquidation. So, she overcame her fears through knowing and purpose. She had a picture of the possibility because the stores were working, but they were just loaded up with so much debt that the company could not pay its vendors. Then the moment came, as Linda explained to me:

"We had to petition the court for cash collateral and the ability to reorganize. This was a big risk, because once you file, then you will have a hearing.

When the hearing happens, it's in the judge's hands whether or not he'll grant you the ability to reorganize, or whether he'll just order liquidation.

"So here's what happened. I called each of the vendors, and I said, 'If you will write a letter stating that you want us to have the ability to reorganize, and that you will grant us terms, in other words you will grant us credit, we will have a chance with the court.'

"I walked into that courtroom with twenty-six letters in my hand. That had never been done before, because companies just don't come out very well in Chapter 11. There were three chairs on the witness stand. I was white-knuckling it the whole way, and I knew the bank would say, 'Frederick's owes us that money.' Once they called it an institution, it gave us a shot at reorganizing.

"First we presented the vendor letters. There were 1,800 families who would be out of work, many of whom were there, and about twenty-five companies that would be severely hurt."

Since their organization was ruled an American Institution and a part of our heritage, the judge was able to rule in her favor and Linda, against tremendous odds, saved Frederick's of Hollywood from liquidation. She knew the right answer, and painted a compelling picture of why the organization should continue. She built commitment in her employees, her vendors, and finally in the bankruptcy judge. She demonstrated tremendous courage to confront her fears and the fears of the team. She knew what was right and never gave up.

Earlier in the book I discussed how Tim Pulido, president and CEO of Campero USA and Pollo Campero International, had turned around Shakey's Pizza by remodeling the stores. These remodels cost millions of dollars, which took great courage to spend, on the hope that sales would increase. When I asked Tim about this he told me:

"Even though the living vision of our model stores indicated the formula for success, people at all levels in the organization needed the courage to change behaviors that they had gotten used to. It takes courage to let go of something you know and try something new. Essentially, you have to admit you were wrong, and then you have to go through the clumsy period of trying new ways. Then you have to polish your act.

"We really had to stand up to our peers on the executive team and say 'Look, we acknowledge that we made a mistake and we need a new course.' I'm telling you there were people who did not want to accept that change, and that was a tough one. People would say 'Who the heck do you think you are? We've got a lot of proud people here, and they work.' It was an outstanding team. It took time for us to acknowledge reality."

His knowledge of the business led to wisdom, but the final call was an intuitive one later confirmed by the data.

Never, Never Give Up

When a leader knows the answer, he or she never gives up. Even with shortening product cycles and limited capital, leaders must first define the markets, enter them, and create excitement. With targeted actions that everyone believes in, the leader forms "FastBreak Action Teams" that are infused with clarity and confidence to reach the new reality.

Even with good marketing and branding in the marketplace, business leaders will still need courage. Most give up on canned consulting programs because they do not really know the answer. They are just putting in a process that worked in other companies. Once the answer to a strategic problem is understood, you have to build a specific approach in order to successfully implement.

Of course, responding to market changes is easier said than done, but if you can take the time to follow and do the preparation I have discussed, you can take full control of your future. Fears and doubts arise during each phase of strategic change, and a leader must work to mitigate those. Developing a compelling picture of the future state is important, but you must continue to build commitment to the changes that will be required because when things get tough, people give up and go back to what they have been comfortable with, no matter how clear the opportunity.

A Lesson from History

During World War II, the Nazis had rolled over Europe, destroying great armies and cities, killing millions of innocent people. But Winston Churchill, with his army defeated at Dunkirk, his air force in tatters, and with German U-boats sinking his navy and blocking supply lanes, had the courage to say, "We will never surrender." He did this with the full knowledge that he and his family would be tortured and killed should Hitler win.

Addressing his divided government and the nation in 1940, two years before the United States joined the fight, he painted a clear and compelling picture of the mission while acknowledging reality:

> "I would say to the House, as I said to those who have joined this government, I have nothing to offer but blood, toil, tears, and sweat. We have before us an ordeal of the most grievous kind. We have before us many, many long months of struggle and of suffering. You ask, what is our policy? I can say: It is to wage war, by sea, land and air, with all our might and with all the strength that God can give us; to wage war against a monstrous tyranny, never surpassed in the dark, lamentable catalogue of human crime.

> "That is our policy. You ask, what is our aim? I can answer in one word: It is victory, victory at all costs, victory in spite of all terror; victory, however long and hard the road may be; for without victory, there is no survival. Let that be realized. No survival for the British Empire, no survival for all that the British Empire has stood for, no survival for the urge and impulse of the ages, that mankind will move forward towards its goal. But I take up my task with buoyancy and hope. I feel sure that our cause will not be suffered

to fail among men. At this time I feel entitled to claim the aid of all, and I say, 'Come then, let us go forward together with our united strength'."

Worthwhile business or personal missions are not this dramatic or important, but the courage and clarity represented in this moment in history is a great model for any leader. Practicing the process to invent the future will make teams stronger, more confident, and more effective in enhancing their company's performance in the marketplace. Each leader who creates opportunities grows the wealth of the company, the people within it, and the communities they touch. Look back on the successes in your life and you will see these steps.

Synchronizing with Reality

Genius is synchronizing with reality, as opposed to synchronizing with ignorance. Ignorance is unawareness of knowledge or information that is critical to success in the moment. Ignorance is being disconnected with or not understanding the reality of the moment. Genius rises from a deep unfiltered awareness of the realities of the moment.

Every moment flows with causes and effects that have powerful momentum. This stream extends into the future. It cannot be dramatically changed once in motion, but like the surfer riding a wave, you can combine its energies with your own to maximize the performance of a business or a life. Ignorance, or lack of awareness of reality, always results in being left behind, as reality flows forward. Some would say that the financial crisis and the failure of some American auto companies are examples of this.

A leader must learn to live synchronized with the flow of cause and effect, which I call Integrative Presence. Thoughts and actions that arise from this connection are genius, and have caused most of extraordinary achievements in business and the world. The aware leader knows the difference between the feeling of being synchronized with ignorance, which is often caused by connection to thoughts and concepts that feed one's ego or are no longer true, and the clear powerful feeling of genius.

When you understand this, it becomes important to collaborate and synchronize your efforts with others who can live Integrative Presence. It's confusing at best to collaborate with people who are not unleashing their genius in this manner, and are for the most part ignorant of present reality. Great leaders form networks with and synchronize with those who have this level of awareness. They build and develop teams around them whose insights come from synchronizing with present reality. Because of the warp-speed pace of change, any activities outside of this approach are going to lead to failure in the 21st century. Teams of people synchronizing with reality through Integrative Presence will succeed at levels that are presently beyond our imaginations.

The Twilight Club

The Twilight Club was an organization founded in the late 19th century, during another time of peril, with the intention of countering the moral decline of society by bolstering spiritual and ethical awareness. The club met in the evenings at members homes in the U.S. and England, hence the name. Its members were business leaders, philosophers, political leaders, and poets who infused wisdom into business, government, and science, creating breakthroughs that benefit us today. Members in England and America included James Howard Bridge, John Burroughs, Andrew Carnegie, Robert Collier, Calvin Coolidge, John Dewey, Sir Arthur Conan Doyle, Ralph Waldo Emerson, Richard Watson Gilder, Oliver Wendell Holmes, Henry Holt, Rudyard Kipling, Edward Markham, Mihajlo Pupin, Theodore Roosevelt, Walter Russell, Herbert Spencer, Mark Twain, Cornelius Vanderbilt, and Walt Whitman.

What we do today will affect the future generations of this millennium, as The Twilight Club affected our time. Our goal should be to get the best hearts and minds together to help invent our future.

Join the World Leadership Forums

I propose we gather thought leaders again, in what I call the World Leadership Forums, as a contemporary update to the Twilight Club. As western society matures, and faces competition from emerging countries, it is time to call on those who seek wisdom to look deeply at where we are today. It seems we have lost the moral and spiritual spark that built our country and the western world. It is time to question our assumptions and create a new free-enterprise system based on a common purpose that will again be a role model of freedom and prosperity for our time.

Those who are concerned about the direction of our world, have influence, and bring a strategic understanding of the flow of events should consider joining the World Leadership Forums. As our membership grows, forums will form in each major city. Forums will be connected virtually to maximize insight and action. Each will act both locally and globally to set the foundations of a more ethical, spiritual, and innovative world. Each forum will meet on its own schedule for deep reflection and dialog to discover answers to the complex problems facing our society. Our purpose together is to change the direction of our country, whose moral and spiritual leadership has taken a back seat to greed, selfishness, and power.

It took courage for Winston Churchill to stand up to the most powerful military on earth, and it took courage for the members of the Twilight Club to propose and implement innovations such as the Boy Scouts of England and America and the Better Business Bureau. I am asking you to join this discussion and to be a member of the World Leadership Forums.

Here is a link to The World Leadership Forums group on Facebook. I hope that you will join in the dialog, and possibly form a group in your city. 🔗

PRACTICES and ACTIONS

"We have nothing to fear but fear itself." —**Franklin Roosevelt**

1. **Notice Your Fears:** As things do not go the way you have planned, before you give up, notice the nature of your fears and write them in your journal. For example, here are some of mine:

- Who am I to write a book?
- People do not care what I think.
- This is too much work.

It is important to know your own fears, because they will come up over and over again in different forms. When you can see through their masks, you can see through to the fear, and dismiss them, as is discussed in Susan Jeffers' book, *Feel the Fear and Do It Anyway.*

2. **Go Back to Your Intention:** As fears come up, go back to your intention and read the statement you wrote about that described your compelling picture for the future in Chapter 6. Write that purpose down again you your journal.

3. **Never Give Up:** When I get dressed to take a twenty-two-mile bike ride, my mind will often start saying things such as:

   - It is too cold.
   - I am tired.
   - It will not hurt to skip a day.

But I do my best not to listen to these excuses. Whatever you want to accomplish, each day, each month, each year, and in your life, never give up.

Write down the typical excuses you make when things get tough, and learn to dismiss them. Let your vision and commitment for the future you know is right for you wipe away your fears.

PART SIX:

MASTER INNER STILLNESS

Photo: Sarah Clarehart

Chapter 14

Achieve Command Presence

At the center of the most powerful storms on earth is stillness. This calm organizes the energy. When the eye of the hurricane breaks up, so does the power of the storm. The same is true for each of us. Inner stillness helps us organize and manifest our dreams and actions. This is called command presence.

Photo courtesy of NASA

"Be calm and centered before you make decisions."
—Casey Sheahan, Former CEO, Patagonia

"I just want to be proud of the place where we work. I want everyone to be respected and trusted, and do a great job. I know that stress damages people and their performance, and I do everything to eliminate stress. I want people to have a nice, quality life. I try to build a drama-free zone."
—Kristen Allison, CEO, Burnham Benefits

"Certain people are consumed by what is in front of them, and others, in moments of stillness, can see beyond to what could be."
—Larry Senn, Founder and Chairman, Senn Delaney Leadership

"We are shaped by our thoughts: We become what we think. When the mind is pure, joy follows like a shadow that never leaves."
—Buddha

Photo: Sarah Clarehart

Have you ever been talking to someone and realized that you were not there for a good part of the conversation, until that person asked you a question? Where do we go? For me, I get lost in my thoughts. If I am concerned about something "important," thoughts about that concern will repeat over and over again in my head. If you happen to be talking to me at that time, I will not hear, or really even see you. We have all experienced these moments.

I have also experienced those moments when I was totally present, living within a good book, playing sports, or leading a dialog that suddenly opened into insight and consciousness. When in this state of presence, I know what people will be saying before they say it, and I will respond spontaneously with probes and questions that expand our mutual consciousness.

Experience Clarity

When I am "in the zone," responding to "the slings and arrows of outrageous fortune," I sense an inner stillness that wipes away unnecessary fears. Take time to recall times in your life when everything seemed to work, when you were "in the zone," or just slipped into a peaceful state. When that happens to me, I feel my attention moving from my thoughts to the present moment, and know exactly what I am doing. The peace gives me insight into what is happening moment to moment. It is like the veil of my thoughts lifts and I can see things that I had never seen before.

An old Tibetan Buddhist story called "The View" illustrates my point. It's about a man who lived on top of the greatest mountain, with no windows and doors. No light ever came in, until one day a crack in one wall let the sunlight through. At first he was scared. "What is this light and why is it coming into my space?" he wondered. But after a while he started looking out through the crack, poking at it. Suddenly the roof lifted and the walls fell down. "WOW, what a view," the man exclaimed ... and it had been there all the time. The walls symbolize our thoughts about the world and the fears they produce. The lifting of our thoughts allows us to see the world as it actually exists.

James Hillman calls this "Proust's stumble." When crossing a courtyard, Marcel Proust stumbled on an uneven paving stone, and suddenly an oppressive blue mood that had come over him lifted like the walls in the Tibetan Buddhist story: "A profound azure intoxicated my eyes, impressions of coolness, of dazzling light, swirled around me." Proust could see the world as it was, undistorted by his blue mood.

Inner stillness opens our consciousness so we can feel the life force that resonates within each of us to a greater or lesser extent. The extraordinary results that come out of dancers or athletes who are "in the zone" happen because they are totally present while being driven by an intention to create something greater than themselves. They respond naturally to the flow of the game or the flow of life. There is a knowing and grace to their actions. Why?

Information Flows to Us

As I mentioned in *Unleashing Genius*, science has proven that a force connects all forms of consciousness. Science has also discovered that communication along this network is beyond space and time. Therefore, in every instant, information flows into us and out of us without any need for thoughts or beliefs. This information ripples throughout the universe. Animals are an example of living beings that use this network. Birds migrate thousands of mile and return to the same nest in the spring. Fish go out to sea and spawn up the same river in the same place. Animals can do this in part because they do not have thought interfering with their perception. While we have gained a lot from thought, it seems we have lost touch with our instincts.

A rhythm and flow occurs as various energies are released and affect each other. The exact response to any action is best executed with a high level of consciousness. Many stories about this experience say it often comes without warning, but more often when the person or team has an openness to the possibility of it happening. It will expand the level of play in sports or life, adding dramatically to the level of practice, muscle memory, and preparedness.

Master Presence

A professional baseball hitter knows the importance of mastering presence—that any distraction will interfere with using a skinny bat to hit a small, round ball traveling at 90 miles per hour. You may say, "Well, I am not a professional athlete," but I am sure you strive to master something.

Perhaps you enjoy being in service to people, and have built a career around that. In whatever way you chose to earn a living, mastering presence not only improves your performance dramatically, but also provides a mutual experience of mastery. Our presence lifts other people's presence. Mother Teresa or the waiter in your local restaurant providing deep presence at any moment improves your effectiveness. Being in service to others is a noble purpose, in whatever form it takes.

Without being consciously connected to the present moment, over time the experience of hearing only our own thoughts circling around in our heads becomes normal. When we, and the people around us, are painfully distracted by our thoughts to the exclusion of what's actually happening around us, it seems like it is just the default state for humanity. Stress is on the rise while violent crime is at an all-time low. According to the book *The Better Angels of Our Nature,* violent crime is down 65 percent in the U.S. and across the world since the 1960s, while reporting of crime is up dramatically. This Increase is creating a false reality. We are frightening ourselves.

The problem is this: We often think our thoughts are real, and then, to make it worse, we hang out with people who agree with us. The tribe reinforces our thoughts about reality. "Group think" becomes a cultural trance, which creates high levels of distortion. If we are present, we can break through the barrier of our thought to a deeper, more meaningful reality. Seeing the flow of cause and effect without massive distortion from our thought is mission-critical for anyone trying to invent their future.

Breaking Out of the Trance

We have all gotten caught up in some form of a cultural or family trance. I found that I could not truly become myself until I broke away from my family trance, which was "come to America and become rich and famous."

During the Renaissance, the emergence of science upset the cultural trance of its day. Its innovators had to let go of what they thought they knew and challenge the status quo. People were burned at the stake for challenging cultural trances.

I would not blame you for being afraid to challenge everything you have learned. People in your circle might think something is wrong with you. Today you may not be burned at the stake, but might be banished from your tribe or family. There is a lot of bad history concerning those who have tried to invent a better future. But the only way to discover new realities is to let go of what you think you know, and find yourself in the present moment.

What complicates this approach is that we hate to be wrong. What helps is to have people in our lives who challenge us and support us in discovering new realities.

Let Go

When you are distracted by your thoughts and beliefs, you can easily miss the songs of the angels playing full blast. Then, when by some accident you hear a chord, it seems supernatural. But the truth is that these divine songs are always there in the stillness. Life is beautiful beyond all description, but most of us are lost in our thoughts and fears which are only approximations of the reality we experience.

It seems that all our atoms glow brighter when they are in tune with this force. When we consciously dance to its rhythm, a life of flow is beyond description, like a chain of blissful moments running through your being, or the wonder of a moment between two friends that brings us to tears.

All that is needed to create this state is to let go of the thoughts that are captivating your consciousness. Then this natural rhythm and flow expands your field of perception. How do you know which thoughts and beliefs to let go of? Start with the ones that are making you feel bad about yourself.

Natural States of Mind

Natural, inborn, innate states of mind were identified in a landmark study by a group of psychologists, and addressed in the book, *Sanity, Insanity and Common Sense*. One of my friends, Greg Stewart, read my book *Unleashing Genius*, and put together a list of his own.

When we let go of beliefs and thoughts that create a negative state of mind, the following states naturally arise. Thoughts can only point to the possibility of these state of mind, only letting go of them can allow the experience.

Peaceful	Here/now presence
Trusting	Awareness
Limitless	Gratitude
Wellbeing	Courage
Expansive	Patience
Risk taking	Gentleness
Curiosity	Connectedness
Natural knowing	Abundance attitude
Agape love	Compassion
Open	Empathy
Infinite possibilities	Kindness
Accepting and allowing	Negotiation
Care and concern	Forgiving

Constructed States of Mind

The following states of mind are constructed from our ego's need to protect us psychologically. They come from childhood wounds that tend to create distorted beliefs and comparative circular thoughts that circle in our heads and block our perception. In fact, repeated circular thoughts are what leads to insanity. We become trapped in limited solutions and distorted realities that block out universal intelligence.

Angry	Prideful
Self-protective	Blaming
Constrictive	Feelings of powerlessness
Safety centered	Hatred
Only self needs matter	Fearful
Automatic reactions	Narrow view of reality
Restricted range of solutions	Ego mind and heartless
Black-and-white thinking	Rationalizing
Defensive	Attacking
Judgmental	Shame-based
Self-preservation	Feeling isolated
Feeling victimized	Withdrawn
Self-doubt	Projection
Endless fighting	Vengeful

When you find yourself here, you need to look deeply for the constructed beliefs that distort your view of reality and keep you from the natural and positive states of human consciousness with which we were all born.

As I've said before, the thoughts and beliefs we develop are at best an approximation of reality. Drop them when you can, ignore them if they persist, because they block you from the present moment and feeling positive human consciousness. When you let go of these constructed states, you will naturally rise to your inborn states like an athlete slipping "into the zone."

Letting go, of course, is easier said than done because our egos are always on watch. Unfortunately, it can draw only on past experiences, and many of our reactions to these experiences were distorted by the emotions and concerns of the moment. The key to transcending the ego and letting go is knowing the difference between the actual flow of cause and effect, and our thoughts and beliefs about it. You may ask, how do I know the difference between feelings that come from my thoughts and feelings that come from the flow. Of course it takes practice, but the simple answer is if you are in one or more of the constructed states of mind listed above, the feeling is coming from some combination of thoughts. You do not have to know exactly what the thoughts are to let go of them. As these negative states of mind arise practice letting them go.

In combination with practicing letting go, you have to practice living in the natural higher states of mind. As I have said earlier, meditation, cycling, music and any number of activities lead to these states of mind. Choose one or two that work for you, and make it a routine to be in the state of presence. Over time, being in constructed states of mind will seem uncomfortable and you will start to automatically let go of them.

Our thoughts can either point the way to possibility or block us from our natural grace and ease. As my old Yorkshire grandpa said when I was trying with all my might to be right, "You wouldn't see the rabbit if it jumped on your face, lad." He told me this just after I had let a great opportunity go by.

Kristen Allison: Interview

Here is a practical example of letting go of circular thoughts. Earlier in this chapter, I discussed cultural and family trances. Sometimes a culture in an organization can help you let go of your thoughts and stimulate creativity. Kristen Allison, whose highly successful company, Burnham Benefits, was named "Best Place to Work in Orange County, California," told me this when I asked her about her secrets to success:

> *"I don't take things personally, because it is not about me. It is about everybody. I do not want to be the center of attention. I just want to be proud of the place."*

By letting go of thoughts she might take personally Kristen not only paints a picture of the future culture she wants, but becomes a living example while making everyone safe? If you want to have a better life, business, or community, start with not taking yourself too seriously. It will do wonders for your mood and creativity. Fear narrows your consciousness and activates the primitive parts of your brain designed to protect you from harm. A repeated feeling of safety and purpose expands your consciousness, and helps you let go of fears that have no merit in the present.

As your fears subside, a fountain of creativity flows. This change is as natural as water flowing downhill. Your fears from the past, which are at best approximations of the reality they are trying to describe, will hide present reality. Forgoing frequent contact with the present is like our relationship with water. You can live without if for a while, but without it you will slowly die.

I tend to be hard on myself, as my father was. At some point is my life I realized I was afraid of disappointing myself, a motive that drove me, but also hardened me. I did not want to set my expectations too high. Until I got passionate about a new career, that limiting outlook was a perfect expression of who I was at the time. In taking a personal development course, I realized that helping people feel happier not only was my passion, but I was good at doing so. I moved heaven and earth to get the perfect firm to hire me. Nothing was going to stop me. My intention was in total alignment with my soul's purpose. Then everything changed, and miracles occurred.

Like any form of genius, once discovered, it seems simple. When I asked Kristen again about the key to her tremendous success, she said,

> *"I just say I had a great dad who treated everybody with respect. He really had employees at the dinner table, and he treated them well. They protected him and gave back what they got, and his business was a success."*

How simple this is, when you think about it for a second! Treat yourself with respect, while at the same time taking yourself less seriously. You will be amazed at how you feel. No one else needs to be involved.

I learned a lot in a course called "Sing for Your Soul," led by a dear friend of mine, Frolic Taylor. The first song we learned to sing was Joe Cocker's hit, "You Are So Beautiful." The practice she gave us was to sing the song into a mirror until we truly got it. I remember the moment when I looked back at myself and smiled with a twinkle in my eyes. Everything changed at that moment as I began to see my own inner beauty and genius. I also began to recognize the genius in others.

> *You are so beautiful ... to me.*
>
> *You are so beautiful ... to me, can't you see?*
>
> *You're everything I hope for.*
>
> *You're everything I need.*
>
> *You are so beautiful ... to me*

Here is a YouTube version to inspire you:

I strongly recommend you sing to yourself in the mirror until you get it, and when you do, please join the World Leadership Forums page on Facebook, post your insights, and share your experience.

To successfully invent your future, you must know yourself. Ask yourself what your natural rhythms and gifts are. With the wrong view of yourself, like the Tibetan man in the windowless cabin, you will not see that which is right before your eyes, on the other side of a wall. You will not see your natural genius, and as a climber with a distorted view of a high mountain trail, you might easily slip and fall. Missed steps are almost certain if your thoughts keep you in the dark.

Clear Your Head and Let Life Come to You

As I mentioned previously, NBA star Michael Jordan and his team triumphed when he let the game come to him. Prior to discovering his transformative approach, he was just trying to find more success, doing all the things that got him to where he was. But as I have often told new leaders, "What got you here will not keep you here." The world is constantly changing, so hanging onto old thoughts, patterns, and beliefs will stop working for you sooner or later. All you have to do is let go and your state of mind will move to the present moment, which is where you slip "into the zone."

Again, are you chasing your thoughts about life and overshooting the rhythm and flow? Are you working hard and yet the magic is not happening? Do you wonder why others succeed and don't seem to be working as hard?

Again, ask yourself if you are fully trained in life. Do you understand the game of life, or the endeavor in life you are pursuing?

As I have said before, you have to understand how life works as Michael Jordan understood the game of basketball. Notice whether you are running past opportunities, having to double back, only to find that those opportunities have closed. Stop, and work on becoming centered in yourself and your purpose until you feel the joy of living in your heart. Master each breath, still your mind, and walk as if you are dancing with an invisible lover. The life force is infusing you in every moment, even when you are too busy looking ahead to notice.

Unleash your talent from the chase, and deepen how you live in the present. Then dance with the rhythm and flow as it comes to you, and with a slight move, redirect it. Like magic, your life and life itself will expand.

Finding Stillness and Your Inner Compass

As I stated earlier, the flow of life is like the complex themes, harmonies, and rhythms in music. You need to spend lots of time dancing with those rhythms to know how to influence the flow of the dance. You must dance first with the rhythm and flow of the present, and then lead. There is no substitute for this kind of presence in your life. Whether you are targeting markets in your businesses, playing a sport, or dancing to a good band, being "in the zone" is a blast! The energies of life will feed you, and your creativity will lead the flow of whatever events are happening in your world.

When you do this, your inner stillness attracts your natural intelligence and becomes your inner compass. Your inner stillness reveals the difference between your thoughts about the flow of cause and effect, and the actual flow.

You have to practice to know the difference between the feelings that come from your thoughts and ego, and your natural wisdom. Having the wisdom to access your inner stillness will activate your true compass. Having this compass will then help you walk with the wind of the life force at your back and in your heart.

Here is a poem I wrote that expressed this thought:

Hurricane

At the core of great hurricanes
That lift the sea and blow
Great waves over the land
Is deep stillness

As the stillness grows
So does its circling power
Releasing roaring trains
Of cyclonic energy
Washing away structures
We hold onto instead of life

As will your foolish thoughts

That destroy your peace

Be swept away by Wisdom

If stillness grows within

The center of yourself"

Excerpt From: Paul David Walker. "A Glimpse of My Poetic Collection."

PRACTICES and ACTIONS

Achieving happiness and wisdom through inner stillness is so simple, almost too simple to believe. Here are the steps:

1. Realize that your thoughts are only an approximation of reality, not reality itself.

2. Learn to observe and be amused by your thoughts. Don't take them seriously. Likewise, don't take other people's thoughts too seriously. They are doing the best they know how.

3. Slow your thoughts down to leave space for the life force to enter your consciousness.

4. Practice letting go of your thoughts, rather than repressing them.

5. Remember experiences in your life that were full of joy, and write them down.

6. Immerse yourself in nature. The trees and oceans are not stressed.

Try these steps to stillness—you will like it.

Chapter 15

Get into the Zone

In moments of stillness, the motion around you slows and you can see, feel, and understand the right course of action. With training, your body will respond. The same kind of stillness is needed as you navigate the whitewater rapids of business—the flow of cause and effect. To see the right way forward, and not get carried away by the current, you might consider being the stillness in the storm. Take time to be still and reflect. As in martial arts, presence and balance are important. Then, once you're "in the zone," you'll succeed.

"I fundamentally believe that people, given the opportunity, want to be incredibly successful. So, I create an environment that enables them to succeed. I think that's where that inner stillness thrives. Everyone is committed to each other's success and feels safe. There is very little fear or backbiting—just the harmony of our voices."

—Bill McGinnis, CEO, NTS Corporation

A recent study conducted by Gallup indicated that happier employees are significantly more engaged and productive. I have known this and helped companies generate millions of dollars with more-engaged workers. Now Gallup has proven this to be the case. Leaders would be well advised to understand these valuable insights with employees, enabling them to cultivate happiness and wellbeing on a daily basis.

In Chapter 14 I referred to a study described in the book, *Sanity, Insanity and Common Sense*, which discovered that happiness and wellbeing are natural states of mind. All types of suffering are simply conditioned responses to our thoughts. Thoughts that we repeat to ourselves detract us from insight and our natural feelings of joy, love, and gratitude.

When you repeat negative thoughts such as "I'm not good enough" or "This person is an idiot," it contributes to a negative state of mind. When these states of mind become "normal," a cycle of negativity seems all the more real. Focusing on such thoughts will keep you from fully engaging in your life. Instead, I encourage you to think of yourself as an athlete who is "in the zone." As I have noted in previous chapters, the best athletes are able to perform at often miraculous levels because they're completely engaged in the present and don't waste energy on distracting negative or delusional thinking.

Start with the Present Moment

"The life force" creates life and life influences the life force, just as a band creates rhythm and flow. The only way to create the future is to engage, like a dancer, with the rhythm and flow of the present; and by doing so you become a co-creator. It is not about wishing and hoping, as the popular book *The Secret* would suggest. The various rhythms and flows of business markets are subsets of the rhythm and flow of "the life force" that animates everything. Great leaders have discovered and mastered this secret.

How to Slip into the Zone: Seven Steps

When I lead executive teams, I share seven important steps to cultivating greater happiness and wellbeing in themselves and their teams:

1. Thought is, at best, an approximation of reality. Until you know this at a deep level, it will be hard to find any true happiness. Believing your thoughts to be real is like eating the menu instead of the food. Both are real, but there is no comparing the two experiences.

2. Take your thoughts lightly. Thought is both the greatest gift and the greatest curse to humanity. While thought enables us to create great works of art and science, it has also defined and imprisoned those who allow it to define them. Those who learn to treat their thoughts lightly experience greater levels of wellbeing and engagement in life.

3. Pain is telling you to stop something. Pain is a warning sign that something is harmful, like being burned by a flame. Psychological pain has the same purpose, warning people that their thoughts are compromising their health. Practice interrupting thoughts to bring attention back to the present.

4. Let go of your thoughts. Patterns can be difficult to break, but it's possible with practice. Notice both your negative and positive thought patterns and let them go. Effective action starts with reality, not an approximation of reality.

5. Understand your roadmap into wellbeing and happiness. Keeping track of peak life experiences in your journal helps you to re-experience and find your way back into your highest states of mind.

6. Be here now. Learning to be present makes it more likely for you to experience life instead of experiencing your thoughts about life.

Thoughts about the past and the future are only approximations of reality. Living in the present is the secret.

7. There is no substitute for practice. Letting go of thoughts in the moment takes practice. Meditate, jog, walk, or dance—anything to interrupt thought with some kind of practice. Holding onto thoughts destroys happiness and wellbeing.

Sharing these steps with your team can be the first step in addressing the wellbeing issue that affects employee productivity. Practicing these steps on an individual basis can help you lead the way for a healthier, happier workplace—and a healthier bottom line.

Why Does Meditation Improve Performance?

To invent your future, you need to have a clear picture of present reality in order to see cause and effect emerging to make effective decisions. Meditation is a practice designed to clear your mind of stress and distortion, and enable you to experience present reality as it is, as opposed to what we think it should be.

Over time our minds become filled with thoughts and beliefs that were placed there both consciously and unconsciously. We have defined experiences and recorded them as beliefs. Thought patterns have developed over the years, some of which are helpful and others are not. We are bombarded with ideas, advertising, and images from TV and movies that stick in our memories. These thoughts often circle in our minds, causing fear and stress.

All of these thoughts and beliefs are filtered by our mood at the time we experienced them. If we were in a good mood, we tend to record a more positive message. If we were in a bad mood, it will be more negative. When we recall this information, it is also filtered by our mood at the moment of recall. The bottom line is that our minds are full of highly distorted information that is often conflicting.

Meditation helps to clear the mind and leave room in your consciousness to experience the reality of the moment. The flow of cause and effect is highly complex and, to be successful in any endeavor, you need to be able to see present reality with a minimum of filtering from the thoughts and images filling your mind.

When working with teams of engineers, I enjoy asking if anyone has invented a successful time machine. Of course, they always say no. Then I ask, "So you are certain that no one can travel to the past and the future?" They laugh and agree.

Still, there is no reality outside of the present moment. The future is a speculation, and the past is what we have recorded in memory or in writing, which is, as I stated earlier, highly distorted. Yet how much time do most leaders spend traveling to the past and the future in their mind? I would suggest too much. The best leaders realize that being able to live in the present moment is the secret to both personal power and strategic advantage. They learn to see through false realities and connect with true reality.

An Example from Sports

After watching Florence Joyner win the hundred-meter dash, a TV interviewer showed a super-slow-motion playback of her run. She was about equal with the field through the middle of the event, and then she leaped out way ahead to win the race. The interviewer played the run again, and just as she put distance between herself and the field, the interviewer stopped the recording and pointed to the screen and asked, "What happened right here?"

Florence answered, "I just let go."

She stopped thinking about the race and slipped into "the zone" and, of course, her performance accelerated dramatically. She was integrating all her training with the reality of the present. Being able to find our way into "the zone" is as critical for business success as it is for athletes.

Some respond to pressure by "clutching," and thereby reducing perfor-mance, while others slip into "the zone." Michael Jordan was famous for performing better under pressure, as are many successful athletes. As a leader, is this true for you? When the pressure is on, do you call for the ball?

Integrative Presence

Sports coaches realize that if athletes think too much about the past and the future, they will miss the reality of what is happening in the present. The future extends from the present, not from the cognitive frameworks in your mind. Those who can let go of their thoughts will find it easier to integrate their actions with present reality. In business, that is "Integrative Presence."

If an athlete can create this state of mind, so can a leader. If these states of mind that seem to create super-human results can be created in one area of life, they should be able to be created in others. While the environ-ment is right for this kind of performance in sports, it can also happen in the everyday business or personal world. The most effective leaders have mastered Integrative Presence, which unleashes genius in any endeavor.

Integrative Presence, as I define it, is collaboration with the natural flow that extends from the present integrated with the knowledge, inten-tion, and consciousness of an individual or group. Integrative Presence helps you integrate all the realities of the moment simultaneously while combining them with your intention. Those who master this presence will unleash genius within themselves, and their followers, to create new realities once unimaginable.

Business is much more complex than sports, but the state of mind that creates Integrative Presence is as important for all of us as it is for athletes. The best leaders are able to achieve this state at will. In a board meeting or when closing an important deal, the best leaders can be in the present while integrating their knowledge and all the events that are happening around them simultaneously.

Know the Difference

The truth is that anything can cause your conscious mind to let go of comparative thought and find Integrative Presence. It would be impossible to catalog all the experiences people have had. What is important is to know the difference between the two states of mind. Meditation is a practice that will help you find your personal roadmap into this powerful state.

When I have asked people to describe how they feel when they experience Integrative Presence, they say words such as confident, at peace, exhilarated, powerful, graceful, focused, and present. Some report a slow-motion effect.

Kareem Abdul-Jabbar told how the five seconds he had to win the NBA championship with one shot seemed like five minutes. He felt relaxed, as if he had all the time in the world, yet he appeared to move like lightning to the rest of the world—the very definition of Integrative Presence. His creativity, within these few precious seconds, was pure genius. He was integrating the skills he had learned over the years, his desire to make the shot, and the flow of the moment, without interruption from his thoughts.

Most people have experienced this state of mind. The question is what percentage of our life is spent in this state? The art of getting into this state of mind is letting go of thoughts and connecting with the flow of events in the moment. Meditation is practice for your mind and body. An athlete must practice his or her sport; a leader must practice disciplining his or her mind.

PRACTICES and ACTIONS

As in sports, there is no substitute for practice. Knowing how to move from "normal thinking" into Integrative Presence comes from practice. Take time to connect with your peak experiences and observe how you transitioned yourself. Find ways to still your mental chatter and connect with the present, and you will become a much more effective and happier person.

The following is a simple meditation technique that can help you clear your mind. It will help you establish an inner roadmap to stillness, which enables you to flow with present reality.

1. **Find the Right Environment:** Find a quiet place and arrange to have no distractions or interruptions, whether it's a special place in your home or a place out in nature. It is especially important in the first stages of meditation to find the right location. It helps you move toward stillness naturally. Over time you will be able to meditate anywhere, at any time, even as you walk through hallways.

2. **Sit Comfortably:** You want your body to be at ease. Find a comfortable chair and be sure not to cross your arms or legs. Sit up straight so you will not have to move should one of your limbs fall asleep.

3. **Take Three Deep Breaths:** When you take these deep breaths, hold the oxygen in as long as you can on each breath, and let the oxygen out suddenly once you can no longer hold the air.

4. **Breathe Normally:** Return to your normal breathing pattern. Close your eyes and put your attention on your breathing process. Follow your breath in and then out. Notice the rhythm and depth of each of your breaths. Spend two to three minutes just following your breath with your attention.

5. **Imagine a Beautiful Place:** Imagine yourself in a beautiful place in nature. Each time you begin meditating, come back to this place. It will serve as an anchor for peace and help you to relax each time. When you have felt the peace of this place, use it as a background and return your attention to your breathing.

6. **Let Go of Your Thoughts:** As thoughts arise in your mind, do not resist them. Practice observing without processing, and then

letting go of them. You can imagine them floating up into the sky or being absorbed by nature. As you let go, return your attention to your breathing.

7. **Deepen Your Breathing:** After you find your natural rhythm, increase the depth of your breathing. Inhale 10 to 15 percent deeper and exhale 10 to 15 percent deeper. Play with this deeper rhythm until it becomes natural. Continue to let go of thoughts as they arise.

8. **Notice Stillness:** At the moment you fully inhale, just before you exhale, notice that a still point occurs. Likewise, after you have fully exhaled, the same still point happens. One, the inhale, is full and the second, the exhale, is empty. Notice the difference.

9. **Fall into Stillness:** At times when your total focus is on this deeper breathing process, you will notice the stillness inside you. Let your consciousness fall into this stillness. Let go and don't be afraid; it is your destination. Stay there as long as your ego will allow. It might take a number of sessions before you achieve this stillness, but it is worth the practice and discipline.

10. **Open Your Eyes:** After about twenty to twenty-five minutes, gently open your eyes without moving and notice the world around you. Notice your state of mind and journal your experience.

11. **Take This State of Mind with You:** Practice staying with this state of mind as you get up from your chair and walk, focusing on your breathing as before. Find a rhythm between your steps and your breath. Count how many breaths per step until you find a comfortable pace that is a little deeper than normal. This will help you begin to integrate this state of mind into your daily life.

12. **Do Short Meditations:** Once you have mastered this practice you will be able to take a few minutes to clear your mind between meetings or even with short pauses during meetings.

Meditation creates the same state of being that Florence Joyner and other athletes achieve when they are "in the zone." Your consciousness will naturally expand and you will be able to perform more effectively.

Once again, there is no substitute for practice. As you continue to meditate, you will find the quality of your thought improving. You will have great ideas and find it easy to solve problems. Creating this space of stillness within you leads to Integrative Presence or being "in the zone." Meditation is a powerful tool for those who are inventing their future. It helps with idea generation and stress reduction. If you are a leader, you need both to be successful.

With practice, every aspect of our lives will improve. Practice being the stillness in the storm, a person who listens, a person who puts aside personal views and is moving like a basketball player in the zone. Demonstrate real stillness when it comes to the performance part of leadership, in contrast to the bombastic person who is constantly throwing shallow or reactionary viewpoints.

Stillness, and the awareness that come with it, creates wonder and humility. The more we know, the more we see endless possibilities and these create a natural humility. As I have said to many of the CEOs with whom I work, it is hard to criticize humility.

Summary:

Synchronize Your Practices

Waves of change are creating new opportunities for some, and disasters for others. When you master how to synchronize the imperatives discussed in this book, using the present pace of change as an accelerator or sling shot, you enter the power curve. The dynamic is similar to being a surfer on the point on a wave, finding the sweet spot of maximum acceleration.

Synchronize Your Practices

When you integrate this book's practices into your life, you can invent your future with ease and grace. Keep these six key imperatives in mind always:

1. Know Yourself
2. Discover the Answer
3. Paint Compelling Pictures
4. Build Commitment
5. Respond to Reality
6. Master Inner Stillness

These tenets are interrelated. In fact, they are building blocks. If you do not know your natural genius, you cannot know the answer. If you do not know the answer, you cannot paint a compelling picture that people can follow, and your dream will never happen. If you can paint a compelling picture, but cannot inspire commitment in others, you will be alone. If you inspire commitment in others, but fail to respond to the present moment, you will lose your way. Without inner stillness, none of these imperatives are possible. When you integrate them successfully, life is a magical dance of joy and abundance.

Know Yourself

- **Know your natural strengths:** Be sure to test yourself using various personality tests, get feedback and coaching from those that know you well, and design your process for inventing your future around the attributes where you have a natural genius.

- **Structure projects around strengths:** Your team or resources should have strengths that complement yours. Find people who have a natural genius around traits that are your weaknesses.

Photo: Sarah Clarehart

- **Understand strategic advantages:** Each organization or project also has natural advantages and strengths. Analyze why a particular project might be attractive to people. Understand why people would want to be involved in the project or new business.

Discover the Answer

- It is critical that you know the difference between the feeling that comes from your ego, versus the feeling of true wisdom and insight. Practice making this distinction.

- Find knowledgeable people, tell them what you are trying to create, and why, and explain to them what you think the answer is.

- Once you know, go forward with passion and speed. Rally all your supporters and begin painting a compelling picture of the outcomes.

Paint Compelling Pictures

- Be sure your compelling picture describes the "why" of your vision. Why is your vision right and who will benefit from making it a reality?

- Illustrate what has to happen when your plan is in place. Describe how things will be different and what people will experience.

- Describe how your vision will come to be, detailing how you are going to accomplish your goal and how people around you can help.

Inspire Commitment

- Most people can hold onto a mildly complex cognitive framework for a maximum of two weeks. So, you will have to find different ways to get people committed and recommitted to your vision.

- Develop a core group of people who are committed and give them talking points to assist you in building commitment.

- Be sure the compelling pictures of this outcome change as outside events change. Do not change what you know to be true, just find new and different reasons to become committed to this picture.

Respond to Reality

- The flow of cause and effect can change at any moment. A competitor can enter the race, the environment can change. Keep your eye on potential future events as they emerge.

- As trends that might get in the way emerge, do what you can to navigate around them, but keep the outcome in mind.

- Do not give up on what you know is the answer, and always find different paths to the outcome, like a basketball player driving to the basket to score. Expand your picture to include changes that may be occurring beyond your control.

Master Your Inner Stillness

- A busy mind can barely see beyond its noise. The flow of cause and effect becomes distorted by too many doubts and considerations.

- Practice clearing your mind of extraneous thoughts and beliefs. Meditate, run, cycle, swim, or do whatever you need to do for the sake of this practice. Develop practices that maintain a deep inner stillness.

- Always be the stillness in the storms that will come. Even when you are not sure how to respond, let people see you are calm and collected. Stillness lets you function in more powerful and relevant ways.

There Is No Substitute for Practice

All of the preceding takes practice, as with mastering anything. Practice each of these steps on smaller projects until you achieve some form of mastery before you take on big projects. Develop your confidence, but never skip these steps. It takes all of them to assure success.

Join the World Leadership Forums page on Facebook to get advice from me and others who are in the process of inventing their future. No one has ever succeeded on his or her own. The greatest leaders have thousands of friends and contacts who can help them. Never burn bridges, but always build them, even if they might appear to lead to nowhere. You never know what opportunities might arise. 🔗

My challenge to you is to practice, and do not listen to the voices in your head that say things such as "I am not good enough" or "Others who have built successful futures have been lucky." Remember what my grandfather said to me: "Luck is when preparation meets with opportunity." This is your chance to prepare for the future you want to create. As you prepare, you will notice opportunities that you might have missed without the preparation and intention. As Louis Pasteur once said, "Chance favors the prepared mind."

Don't forget that there is no substitute for practice on the road to mastering anything. If you have not done so, go back to the sections at the end of each chapter in this book and practice even more.

PRACTICES and ACTIONS

Never forget, there is no substitute for practice. Each of these exercises enhances the others. The next challenge is to integrate these practices into your life seamlessly. Know each one so well that you do not need to think about it consciously. Imbed each one into your consciousness at whatever level you can, and practice deepening your mastery of each.

When these practices seem to flow naturally, work on integrating them together. First try them on small challenges and then try them on more complex parts of your life. Each of us has a natural rhythm and flow. Each of us resonates with our calling and others who share similar callings.

Practice synchronizing these practices into the harmony and flow of your life to enhance any activity you choose.

These practices are how successful lives have been built for thousands of years. They can launch your business or deepen your experience of life by continuously connecting you with your natural genius; helping you to become "the person God meant you to be."

It all waits for you. Play is all you have to do. Let go of what you think you should do and dance with the heartbeat of your life. Resonate with your purpose and with those who share similar dreams. Commit to others' successes and form a vortex of intention. Change your life. Change the world. Invent your future!

"May you realize that the shape of your soul is unique, that you have a special destiny here, that behind the facade of your life there is something beautiful, good, and eternal happening."

— John O'Donohue